A. R. Hope Moncrieff

The Pampas

A Story of Adventure in the Argentine Republic

A. R. Hope Moncrieff

The Pampas
A Story of Adventure in the Argentine Republic

ISBN/EAN: 9783743322479

Manufactured in Europe, USA, Canada, Australia, Japa

Cover: Foto ©ninafisch / pixelio.de

Manufactured and distributed by brebook publishing software (www.brebook.com)

A. R. Hope Moncrieff

The Pampas

'THE PAMPAS:'

A STORY OF ADVENTURE IN THE ARGENTINE REPUBLIC.

BY A. R. HOPE,

AUTHOR OF 'STORIES OF WHITMINSTER,' 'MY SCHOOLBOY FRIENDS,'
'STORIES OF SCHOOL LIFE,' 'STORIES ABOUT BOYS,'
'GEORGE'S ENEMIES,' ETC.

ILLUSTRATED BY 'PHIZ,' JUNIOR.

WILLIAM P. NIMMO,
LONDON: 14 KING WILLIAM STREET, STRAND;
AND EDINBURGH.
1876.

PREFACE.

THE following story has been written with the view of giving a picture of colonial life as it really is, and in the hope that this may be found no less interesting than the sensational narratives which let some readers suppose that they have only to step over the frontier of humdrum civilisation to enter upon a chronic life of excitement kept up by absurd adventures and impossible escapes. At the present day, when so many young men are looking towards the new fields of enterprise offered in abundance by the New World, it is believed that such a work, showing the actual troubles, dangers, and amusements of a settler's life, may prove useful as well as entertaining.

It is possible that these pages may meet the eye of some one who, ten years or so back, made part of the little colony in the neighbourhood of 'Villa Grande,' and who will perhaps recognise certain of the scenes and incidents here portrayed; in this case, attention is called to the way in which the author has dealt with names and other features that might give offence to persons concerned or their friends; and at the same time, all readers familiar with the language, the local names, etc., are requested to accept his confession that he is conscious of inability to take honours at any native 'Spelling Bee.' Pains have been taken, however, to ensure all substantial correctness, and to give a correct description of the scenery, customs, drawbacks, advantages, and adventures in a country in which many Englishmen, for more than one reason, must take a considerable interest.

A. R. H.

April 1st, 1876.

CONTENTS.

CHAPTER I.
	PAGE
THE PAMPAS,	1

CHAPTER II.
A BAD NIGHT AND A BUSY DAY,	18

CHAPTER III.
A RIDE AND A STORY,	34

CHAPTER IV.
LAS BISCACHERAS,	54

CHAPTER V.
UNWELCOME GUESTS,	72

CHAPTER VI.
A JOURNEY UP THE COUNTRY,	93

CHAPTER VII.
OUR CHRISTMAS DINNER,	115

CONTENTS.

CHAPTER VIII.
A PARTY IN CAMP, ... 134

CHAPTER IX.
A NEW YEAR'S DAY, ... 164

CHAPTER X.
LIFE ON THE CAMP, ... 180

CHAPTER XI.
THE INDIANS AGAIN, ... 202

CHAPTER XII.
THE CHASE, ... 221

CHAPTER XIII.
THE PLAGUES OF THE PAMPAS, ... 253

CHAPTER XIV.
CARNIVAL AMUSEMENTS, ... 271

CHAPTER XV.
A CAMP FIRE, ... 286

CHAPTER XVI.
CONCLUSION, ... 298

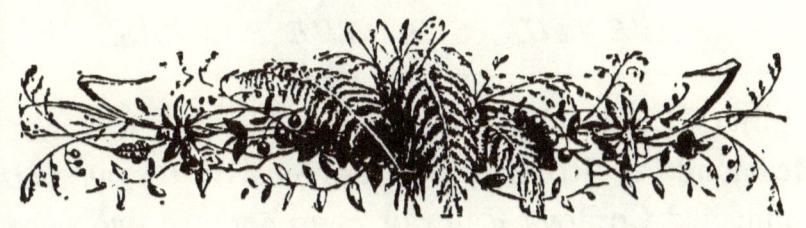

SCENES AND ADVENTURES ON THE PAMPAS.

CHAPTER I.

THE PAMPAS.

WELL do I remember the morning when first I found myself on the Pampas of South America! It was about ten years ago. I had been ill, and was recommended a complete change of scene and occupation for some time; so I gladly accepted an invitation to spend the winter with my cousin, Desmond Butler, and his partner, a Scotchman of the name of Eckford, who had lately gone out together to the Argentine Republic, and were trying to establish themselves as sheep farmers in the province of Cordova.

After a long, wearisome sea journey, a hot, dusty week in Buenos Ayres, and a sail up the river

Parana in a cranky, crowded steamboat, I had met Desmond at Rosario, the terminus of the as yet unfinished Cordova Railway; and here we two were in the train, puffing and rattling along the single line of rails that stretched straight as an arrow across the flat, silent plain, till the eye was tired of watching its track.

It was November, but what a November! Not a breath of wind stirred the vast level of dry grass, which on either hand was bounded only by the hot haze, save for which the blue sky was as undimmed as in the richest English June. We, seated by special favour of the conductor among some horse furniture on an open truck and in the shade of the next carriage, did not feel the heat so much, and looked about at our ease on the scene around us, a scene which to me at least was as yet wholly unfamiliar, and nothing but delightful. There was nothing but the telegraph posts to remind me of crowded, foggy, busy old England; and even they were made of the stems of palm trees, already much worn by the rubbing of cattle, who seemed to think that these posts had been erected for their special gratification.

The cars of the train were of the American fashion, open throughout, with a small platform at each end, on which a few of the passengers stood and smoked. These passengers appeared to be of every nation and occupation, from a German missionary going to visit a community of his countrymen, to an Italian organ-grinder, who was on his way to practise his profession at Cordova. The natives of the Republic were perhaps in the minority among this motley crew, and they might be known either by their picturesque dress or by the extraordinary gravity of demeanour which they maintained in this novel experience of life. The railway was a new thing among them; and though it is not their nature to express surprise, it was plain that they did not as yet know what to say or think of it, utterly foreign as it must have seemed to all their ways and institutions.

Already I had found out the motto of this people,—the phrase which, always on their lips, is a true index to their character. Ask an Argentine any question whatever, and the chances are that, with a shrug of his shoulders, he will reply, '*Quien sabe!*'—'Who knows?' 'What time of day is it?'—'*Quien sabe!*' 'What sort of weather are we going to have?'—'*Quien sabe!*' 'When shall we do so-and-so?'—'*Quien sabe!*' 'What party is likely to get the upper hand in the Government?' —'*Quien sabe!*' So it is not to be wondered at that a railway which is an emblem of punctuality, unweariness, and exact performance of duty, should be to the Argentines a thing strange and even suspicious; or that, when we asked at the hotel in Rosario when the train left, we received at first the familiar reply—' *Quien sabe!*'

On we go, with perhaps an hour's journey from station to station, and sometimes not a house or scarcely a tree to break the monotony for miles. But to me all is new and exciting. Now we pass an *estancia* with its square tower and garden; now a mud hut or two, from which a native woman, brown baby in arms, comes out to stare at the train. The grass is for the most part long and coarse and dry; but here and there, over a tract which has been burned, it is sprouting soft and green, and large patches of the ground are bright with passion flowers, verbenas, and other gaily-flowering plants which I did not recognise. Then would come a *laguna*, or shallow lake, half dried up, the mud at the edge white with a saline deposit. In the distance we catch sight of a vast flock of sheep; two or three graceful deer bound away at our noisy approach; a herd of cattle has strayed upon the line, and the beasts stand stupidly huddled right in the way of the train, paying no attention to the screaming whistle, and only rush off just in time to escape the cowcatcher of the engine. One silly calf chases the train, mistaking it, apparently, for its mother. And scarcely has it dropped off in despair, when another unfamiliar incident of travel calls our attention. An ostrich is on the line; it scurries away in front of the engine, now zigzagging from side to side, now going straight forward between the two rails, but in its terror and stupidity keeping always on the track. The passengers in the front car crane their necks out of the windows to catch sight of the sport. A little Frenchman claps his hands, and screams for delight.

'Two to one on the ostrich!' shouts an Englishman.

'I guess I'll back the locomotive!' replies a Yankee.

Shouts and laughter come from every car from which a view can be had of the chase. The excitement increases; the engineer puts on steam, or slackens, managing always to keep just behind the ostrich, which flies wildly on. At last it flags and swerves, then, just as the train is upon it, rolls head over heels into the ditch by the side of the line, where it lies still, exhausted and terrified, till we are out of sight and hearing.

After this most of our fellow-passengers retired

inside, or picked out the shadiest corners of the platforms of the cars; and there was a general tendency to drowsiness, for the heat now began to be intense. Even the train seemed to be asleep, and to be snoring across this solitude in a strange dream; and I am very much mistaken if the stoker was wide awake. The only thing that seemed lively was the crowd of grasshoppers which peopled the edge of the line, and made their chirping heard above all the noise of the cars.

But Desmond and I had still too much to say to each other; we kept wide awake and chatting till the train stopped at the neat brick station of Villa Grande, where I was to leave this last landmark of civilisation and launch out into the free, wild life of the camp.

Most of my things were coming on by goods train from Rosario. My baggage consisted for the present of a clean shirt, a revolver, a few socks and handkerchiefs, and a box of Holloway's pills. I wore a somewhat shabby shooting-suit, in which, however, Desmond told me I should be thought quite a swell in the 'camp.' He himself, whom I had last seen in Bond Street looking as if he had just come out of a band-box, and stepping cautiously over a crossing not to have his boots stained by the least atom of mud, now wore a ragged old pilot jacket, no waistcoat, a flannel shirt, dirty cord breeches, and long riding-boots, which some one appeared to have been pretending to clean. His little moustache and imperial of old days were exchanged for a big black beard, and the *tout ensemble* was harmoniously completed by a broken straw hat ornamented by a leather thong wound round it.

'*Tempora mutantur*,' I ventured to observe to him, scanning his general appearance curiously, and thinking of an occasion when he would scarcely walk with me through the Park because I had no gloves on.

'Oh, shut up your Greek!' he replied. 'You have to leave that and a good many other things behind you when you come out here. It's all very well for you idle people at home, but we have no time to waste on making ourselves pretty.'

Desmond's travelling equipment consisted solely and simply of a comb and a clean collar, which I carried along with my things in a bundle. With this modest kit we left the station, and made our way into the town, which at that hour had the appearance of being deserted, the inhabitants being at their *siesta*.

Villa Grande, in spite of its pretentious name, turned out to be little better than what we should call a respectable village. There were, perhaps, a hundred decent houses, long low buildings with flat roofs, and gaudily painted walls. These were nearly all bordering upon a large open space, where also stood the church and *cuartel*, or guard-house.

As we strode across this *plaza*, without seeing a human being, except two or three men who were snoring under a great ombu-tree, Desmond pointed out to me the holes of some *biscachos*, a kind of prairie rabbit, which the inhabitants were too lazy to dig out, and which told of a time not long past, when the town consisted of little more than the mud huts that we saw huddled behind the more showy edifices. Everything looked new here; it was the activity produced by the foreign settlers which had called the place into life. I ought to except some fine old orchards and gardens, which delighted my eyes after the continual grass. Watered by little canals, and divided from each other by narrow lanes and hedges, overrun by blue and white convolvuli, they presented a luxuriant glow of peaches, apples, quinces, and figs, that made one's mouth water. One or two fig-trees I saw, which were as large as elms, and quite overshadowed the short, thorny algarobas with their feather-like leaves, that grew so plentifully around them.

We made our way to the post-house, the only place of entertainment in the town, distinguished as such by a group of saddled horses that stood in front, patiently awaiting the pleasure of their masters within. It consisted of two almost unfurnished rooms,—one a 'private' dining-room by day and sleeping-room by night, for the more aristocratic visitors; the other a bar, to which the general run of the customers were restricted.

When we entered we found it occupied by a party of *gauchos*, who seemed to have just awoke, though I soon learned that they are nearly always half asleep, except when on horseback. They were all smoking, which was perhaps just as well, considering the other odours which impregnated the atmosphere of this narrow, low-roofed apartment; and the proprietor, in his shirt and trousers, and a dirty cotton night-cap, was reading out a newspaper for the benefit of the party.

Here I chose to stay while Desmond went round to the stable; for though I did not understand a word of what was going on, I was desirous of seeing something of the natives, and had already got over that impulse of 'new chums,' which leads them to handle a revolver whenever a *gaucho* says good morning to them.

These *gauchos*, the lower class of the original population, are certainly an interesting race, so far as appearance goes. Dark, tall, well-made men for the most part, they wear a dress which gives an effect both of picturesqueness and dignity. They all have *chiripas*, a loose garment like a kilt, tucked in between the legs. Below this some of them wear *calzoncillas*, wide embroidered drawers reaching to the feet, or more commonly, when in working costume, *potro* boots, which are nothing more nor less than the skin of a horse's legs stripped off while still warm and fitted to the man's legs, with an opening for the toes. Their waists are encircled by a broad belt, often profusely ornamented with dollars or brass medals, in which the gaucho carries his knife ; and twined round their bodies they also carry their *boleadores* or *bolas*, cords weighted with balls, which they use with wonderful dexterity for catching animals. Over all is the *poncho*, a wide blanket with a hole in the middle, of gay, not to say gaudy pattern, which hangs in graceful folds over the shoulders. Upon their heads is tied a bright-coloured if not particularly clean handkerchief, and on the top of that they perhaps wear a small straw or felt hat, more for show than use, apparently.

THE POST HOUSE.—*The Pampas*, p. 10.

One could not be long in company of these men without noticing the extreme politeness, and even stateliness, of manner which characterizes them. I was about to light my cigarette, when a ruffianly-looking fellow rushed forward with the match he had just struck, and offered it to me with a grace that might have charmed Lord Chesterfield. I, with British bluntness, must needs decline his aid, showing him that I had a match lit for myself, but he persisted; then I offered him my match, which he declined with a gesture that seemed meant to express his unworthiness; and there we stood bowing and protesting till both the matches burned out and scorched our fingers.

I know I looked very sheepish, but my ferocious friend, not in the least disconcerted, made me a long and eloquent speech, in which he probably desired me to consider everything he had at my disposal, and I have no doubt set me down as a bear for my ungraciousness; but then a great deal of allowance is made by the natives for us Englishmen, who are thought to be mad, though Providence does appear to have favoured us with a strange knack of looking after affairs and making things turn out well. We Britons have many merits of course, but after mixing with foreigners, one can't help wishing that we could add to our business-like virtues something of the ease and suaveness of those races whom we are so ready to look upon as little better than barbarians.

As soon as the horse which Desmond had left here was saddled, we started off for a native *estancia* near the town, where my cousin wished me to spend a day before taking me home, as a great cattle marking was going to take place there,—a scene not to be lost by a visitor to the country. We had only two miles to go, so we agreed to ride and walk by turns,—a plan which Desmond, with his Irish wit, actually imagined would save time! It was only when we had gone most of the way, that he perceived this plan to be the same as walking, so far as speed was concerned.

The heat and the dust were so great, that even my enthusiasm for these novel scenes was overpowered; and I was heartily glad when, after two miles' toiling among the long grass, diversified here and there by a patch of equally luxuriant thistles, we reached the *estancia*. But it was worth any amount of suffering from heat and fatigue, to taste a water-melon as I did, for the first time, at the end of our walk. The round, dark-green globe as big as one's head, the beautiful pink and white pulp, the juice gushing from the wounds! never shall I forget my first introduction to this queen of fruits, and my mouth waters even now, when I remember how the sweet, cool nectar melted away in my parched mouth —it was too sweet a pleasure for this dusty world ; and so enraptured was I, that till my thirst was appeased I scarcely took any notice of the new friends to whom I was now introduced.

The house was a square brick one, containing four or five large airy rooms, opening into each other, and into a verandah or *corridor*, as they call it here, in front. Behind we saw a row of whitewashed huts and sheds thatched with reeds, also, to my great satisfaction, a garden, which looked like a paradise of peaches, nectarines, figs, melons, quinces, pumpkins, and other fruits and vegetables.

Don Pedro, the proprietor, a slender, good-looking young man, received us with great show of attention, and presently two ladies of the family made their appearance, and we all sat down together in the verandah and talked,—that is, the rest talked, and I did my best to catch a word here and there, and to smile pleasantly in answer to the polite and unintelligible welcomes which the señoras showered upon me. Then, while we eat the water-melon which I was in such a hurry to mention, the ladies busied in getting ready *maté*, the Paraguayan tea, which is the great drink of the country. As you will hear a good deal about this beverage, I may as well describe the process of making it at once.

The *yerba* from which it is made, is the pounded leaves and stalks of a plant allied to the holly. A spoonful or two of this is put into a small black pot; a silver tube, called the *bombilla*, with a bulb pierced with holes at the end, is inserted, then hot water and sugar are added. The *maté*-maker first takes a suck at the tube, and when sure that it works all right, hands the apparatus over to the person to be honoured by precedence in drinking. This individual is expected to suck away gravely and deliberately till the liquid part of the contents of the pot is extracted; but if he be a new-comer, he will probably stop to make several wry faces during the operation, both because he does not like it, and because the metal tube soon feels too hot to be held in unaccustomed lips, though, when inured to the practice, he will dispose of the drink with relish, in six sucks and a gurgle. Then the pot is re-filled and passed on to some one else; and as the same pot is always used to go round the company, and some people take three or four turns at it, the process of *maté*-drinking serves to pass away a good deal of time, a fact to which the popularity of the beverage in this lazy country is no doubt largely owing. The natives will take it at any hour of the day, and in any quantity. Some of them seem to live upon it, and upon cigarettes. Strangely enough, these two favourite articles of consumption are spoken of in their language as 'the vices.'

Though we had invited ourselves on this visit, no question was made but that we were to stay the night, and our hosts paid us the unusual compliment of having dinner earlier on our behalf. Breakfast at eleven, dinner at seven, is the rule in such houses; but about six we sat down to a hearty meal, the main point of which was the *asado*—that is, a piece of the loin or ribs roasted on a spit, the favourite dish with high and low. Besides, we had soup, vegetables, and stewed peaches. I did justice to this fare, and, as the stranger, was treated with the greatest kindness and attention; but while enjoying myself, I felt rather nervous lest my ignorance of the language and customs of the country should lead me into some blunder; the more so since Desmond had informed me that our host was nephew to the Governor of the Province, and his wife a daughter of one of the first families in Entre Rios.

But my fears lest I should be found wanting in a due degree of aristocratic elegance were somewhat dissipated when I saw one of the ladies spitting on the carpet, and the other eating so much that she had to undo the front of her dress, and put in a newspaper to cover the opening.

With my cousin as interpreter, I conversed with one of them very satisfactorily, and had the pleasure of telling her that Scotland was not the chief town of England, also that Lord Palmerston was not the king of our country. I soon found that neither instruction nor refinement was a strong point of any class among the natives, polite as they were in their manners.

Dinner was scarcely over before we took to cigarettes, ladies and all. Then we went out for a stroll in the cool of the evening, the pleasantest part of the day. The sun was sinking like a ball of fire, and as soon as his glowing rim disappeared, night began to throw her first shadows on earth and sky. One by one the stars came out in the clear heavens, twinkling as they used to do at home; but you looked in vain for the Plough, and the North Star, and saw instead the four points of the Southern Cross, the brilliancy of which, to my mind, has been very much exaggerated by travellers. There, however, were the Pleiades, and Orion's belt with its three bright stars,—'the Three Marys,' as they are called in South America. And there came the edge of the old moon, the same that looked on me so kindly as we passed

EARLY TO BED.

down the Mersey and saw the last of the Welsh mountains. All was still; no sound to break the silence but the lowing of cattle wending their way to the *corral*, and in the distance the gallop of a horse that brought the last herdsman home from his work. Now that the bustle and excitement of the journey had passed, I was able to realize how far away I was from home, and to wonder if these unfamiliar scenes could ever become as dear to me as the meadows and hedgerows of my native land.

When it was quite dark, and the fire-flies could be seen dancing about among the bushes, we went indoors, and the ladies treated us to some very mournful music on a guitar. But early to bed is the rule here, and on this night there was all the more reason, as to-morrow was to be a busy day. So about half-past nine o'clock we betook ourselves to rest.

CHAPTER II.

A BAD NIGHT AND A BUSY DAY.

N the last chapter I mentioned that I retired to rest, but that was only a way of speaking.

As the stranger, I was shown into the only spare room, furnished with a low camp-bed, a row of wooden chairs, and a spittoon. Here I lay down with only a sheet and a blanket over me, the thermometer being at 80°; and before blowing out the candle put my revolver handy near the bed, a precaution which I thought necessary now that I was out of the range of police courts, not to say that I had scarcely yet got over the boyish feeling of importance in possessing and handling such a weapon. But the only foes I had to fear were not to be repelled by arms of this kind.

I had just got comfortably settled down, and was thinking over the experiences of the day, when I felt a disagreeable itching in my right leg.

'A flea!' I muttered, in my innocence, but very soon became aware that it was not a question of one but of a dozen, who seemed to be feasting all at once on every part of my body. I jumped up and lit the candle, but one glance showed the enemy to be in such force that it was hopeless to think of defence, and I resigned myself to bear the infliction as best I could. But scarcely had I lain down again, when a deep *boom, booming*, gave notice of the approach of a new assailant, and one to which life on board ship had rendered me no stranger. A mosquito! I heard him coming nearer and nearer; I made a dash at him in the darkness with my hand; he retreated, but only to return; and now, horror! there were two or three of them. Then I felt one settle on my face, and it was a positive relief when the sharp needle-like prick told me he had done his work. Now they were booming and buzzing all round me, and I covered my smarting face with the blanket, till the heat became unbearable, and I was obliged to choose between being stifled or stung. So I sat up and began whacking and smacking my face in a fashion which, if I had only been Sancho Panza, would have gone far towards disenchanting the fair Dulcinea; but I rather thought, with envy, of the tailor in the nursery tale, who could kill seven at one blow, whereas in a dozen blows I could only contrive to slay one of my tormentors. And all the while the fleas were hard at it, for my inexperience had let the bed-clothes drop down to the floor, and a perfect army of them had climbed up to the attack on this novel drawbridge.

'This will never do,' I said to myself. 'I must lie perfectly still, and see if sleep won't give me relief.'

I followed out this resolution with great constancy for some little time, resisting the temptation to move about, and checking my wrath towards my persecutors by the philosophical reflection that it 'was their nature to.' My tactics were so far successful that before long I had sunk into a doze, and my mind was filled with strangely mingled fancies of Indians, robbers, revolvers, hunting, and other exciting incidents, when—ah! the dream was gone and I was wide awake, and only too conscious of a sustained and vigorous gnawing at my great toe.

In alarm I leapt up and lit the candle once more, just in time to see three or four disgusting-looking beetles, half an inch long, waddling away from the place where my feet had been. *Benchuchas!*

After this, sleep was out of the question. I could only lie down again and toss about, till I had worked myself up into a feverish and excited state, in which the smallest sound was magnified to my ears.

Some one was snoring loudly in the next room. How I envied the fellow! Cockroaches, or some creatures of the sort, were running up and down the wall in all directions. I could trace their progress quite distinctly, and when I found one making a straight line from the ceiling for my head, my flesh would begin to creep, for I was not aware that they were inside the paper. Again and again I thought there was somebody stirring outside, and put my head out of the window to see nothing, and hear nothing, but the hooting of owls, or the startled footsteps of some small animals rustling among the grass. I walked up and down the room, hoping to tire myself out; but when I lay down, my tormentors went to work again, and sleep seemed further off than ever. Then, striking a light, I tried to quiet myself by studying a Spanish grammar which I had begun to carry in my pocket.

Not a word, however, could I get into my head, and as the light only served to attract mosquitoes into the room, I need not have been sorry when it burned out. Alone and in the dark I was abandoned to the tender mercies of insects, big and little, and had ample reason to understand the saying that the small evils of life are more harassing than the great ones. I know I would rather face a moderate-sized beast of prey, any day, than be shut up with a dozen fleas on a hot night. Talk of Prometheus and the vulture! His fate would have been far more appalling if he had been tied down on a rough, knotty mattress and exposed to the stings of a couple of mosquitoes. 'Luke's iron crown and Damien's bed of steel' should not lightly be exchanged for the insidious gnawing of a *benchucha*. Yet these are sufferings and terrors to which colonists in South America are nightly exposed.

At last, in despair, I got up, partly dressed myself, and lay down on three hard chairs in a row, with my coat rolled up for a pillow. I scarcely hoped to find sleep here, but while I was thinking that it was useless to expect it, sleep must somehow have come upon me unawares, for in an hour or two I was roused up, to feel more uncomfortable and unrefreshed than if I had never gone to bed.

What awoke me was the sound of men shouting and cattle lowing beneath my window. I shook myself out of a dream that I was at home again and that it was market-day, and looking out was aware of hundreds of horned heads and waving tails approaching from all quarters for the great cattle-marking which we had come to witness. Tired as

I felt, it was a point of honour with me to see all that was to be seen; so I dressed and went outside, where, though it was scarcely daylight, I found all in motion.

The whole plain was alive with different herds of cattle wending their way towards the *rodeo* or mustering-place, under the charge of native herdsmen, *peons*, as they are called, who rode behind, and drove the beasts on with short whips, and a peculiar yell, beginning on a high falsetto note and running down the scale. I speak of *beasts*, but I soon learned to use the word *animal*, for Englishmen out there get into the way of translating literally the Spanish terms. Thus a small troop of horses would be called a 'point,' and men always spoke of 'rounding' or 'rounding up' a flock of sheep, or a herd of 'animals.'

When, by dint of shouts and shoves and blows, all were driven to the *rodeo*, there must have been between a thousand and fifteen hundred cattle closely packed together, and from the roof of the house presenting the appearance of a restless sea of horns. Through this surging mass, the *capataz*, that is, the chief *peon*, pushed his way on horseback and saw that all were present,—a task easier than it seemed, as the herds, the numbers of each of which were known, kept together; and I was informed that the *capataz* could tell if ten animals were missing from the whole. In the meanwhile, two or three *peons* kept 'rounding' the *rodeo* to keep them from straying, while the rest, slackening the girths of their horses and letting the reins hang down, gathered round a fire to drink *maté*, and talk till the marking should begin. Curiosity drew me near this scene of chattering and gesticulating, and I was puzzled to see some of the men drawing elaborate figures on the ground, apparently by way of explaining their meaning. On inquiry, I was told that this was their mode of describing an animal they might have seen straying on the camp. Every owner has a registered brand of his own; and though these brands often bear a great resemblance to each other, a native will remember the exact mark on a cow which he fell in with months before.

A large number of visitors were now arriving, for on such an occasion the neighbouring *estancieros* or their servants come to pick out any cattle of theirs which may have got mixed with the herd. So I had an opportunity of observing that our neighbours were likely to be of all nationalities. Besides natives, there were two or three Englishmen, a Scotchman, an Irishman, a German, two Italians, a Dane, and some sturdy-looking fellows that they told me were Basques, a hardy, industrious race, who do very well in this country. If I had been introduced to a Turk or to a Chinaman, I should not have been in the least astonished. And that I might feel at home as soon as possible in this strange gathering, I retired from the bustle to take a look into my Spanish grammar, in which I progressed so well, that at breakfast I was able to say 'good morning' to the ladies with great fluency.

When all was ready, there was a general move towards the *rodeo*. The branding-iron, set in a long wooden handle, was heated in a fire at some distance from the herds. Here were stationed a few old men and boys, on foot, armed with pieces of hide for tying the legs of the poor calves when they had been lassoed and brought up to the branding-place. This, the more honourable and coveted part of the duty, was allotted to the ablebodied *peons*, who galloped about shouting and making their lassos circle over the heads of the cattle, with a grace and skill unattainable by those not to the manner born. One may say that the *gauchos* are almost born to the use of this weapon; for as soon as the children are able to walk, you may see them trying to lasso cats with bits of string, or aiming miniature *boleadores* at ducks and fowls. I have practised the art a good deal; but though I think

I could manage to catch a pump or a stuffed pig, at least once in half a dozen tries, I should be sorry to find my chance of a dinner depending on my proficiency.

The *capataz* now began to direct which animals should be driven out and caught. As soon as a calf was brought to the edge of the vast herd, it was saluted by a chorus of yells and shrieks, quite horrible enough to make it take to its heels. Away goes the poor beast, making for the open camp beyond. But a horseman is galloping after it, and when he gets the side of its head turned towards him for a moment, he whirls the lasso with unerring aim, and flings it round the neck of the calf, which stops suddenly, shakes its head violently, stands with its feet stretched out before and behind, runs to this side and that, perhaps rolls over on the ground, and in every way endeavours to get rid of the lasso. But in vain; the cunning man and his well-trained horse know their work too well. With the lasso fastened to the saddle, he plays the calf as if it were a fish, and before long has brought it close to the fire, where the men on foot are waiting to secure it. The poor animal is probably dead beat by this time; a thong thrown round its hind legs brings it down with a jerk, and it is dragged forward to the fire, where the owner or the *capataz* is ready to imprint the brand on its hip.

Now it is set free, staggers up, looks all round for the rest of the herd, and as soon as it catches sight of them, trots away more frightened than hurt, but is not allowed to go free without the young rascals of boys trying their 'prentice hands at lassoing it with a piece of old rope. This treatment sends it off again into a gallop, and having run the gauntlet of these amateurs, it is at last allowed to join its anxious and sympathetic comrades, whose turn is yet to come.

So the work went on, calf after calf being brought up and branded, and in the meanwhile the rest of the herd were no doubt wondering what it was all about, unless their own previous experiences served to enlighten them. But what with the close packing, the pushing, the lowing, the shouting, the galloping, and the incessant brandishing of whips and lassos, some of the poor beasts began to get very restless; and just as I approached the edge of the crowd on foot, to have a nearer view of what was going on, one old cow was worked up to such a pitch of rage that she broke loose and made a charge into the open with her tail in the air, and her horns looking like mischief. At once the horsemen scattered in all directions with loud cries that only infuriated the cow still further; and pawing the ground and tossing her head, she turned upon me as I stopped short and wondered for a moment what was the matter. But when in a moment more I saw her horns levelled full at me, I stood still no longer. *Corre! Corre!* shouted the *peons*, and there was no knowledge of the language needed to make me understand this advice. I turned and ran as I had never run before, fancying I felt the beast's breath close behind me, and that next second I should find myself flying in the air. The cries and yells redoubled; I flew on, making for a solitary small tree which I saw some hundred yards or so off. There was a peal of laughter mingled with the shouts, which ought to have reassured me, but I never stopped even to look round, till, panting and perspiring, I reached the tree, and made one spring up its gnarled trunk. Ah! the branches were full of thorns, for it was an *algaroba*, and I felt my clothes and my skin torn in a dozen places. At least I was safe, and gaining a branch a few feet above the ground, I looked behind me to see the cause of my flight lying struggling on the ground some way off, with a couple of lassos round her legs. So for about fifty yards I had been running away with nothing behind me, and in the sight of the whole assemblage!

I was deeply ashamed of myself, and not a little lacerated, too, by the prickly branches, from which I descended much more cautiously than I had got up. I durst not face the *peons* again, but made for the corridor of the house, where the ladies were sitting. They, too, received me with a burst of laughter, a sound which is equally intelligible in all languages, and I wished with all my heart that I were back in England again, where cows behave reasonably, and trees are not thorny, as a rule. But though they laughed, the ladies behaved like true women to me in my miserable plight. One fetched a bowl of water to wash my scratches, while another took a needle and thread and did her best to repair my garments. While this was being done, I stayed with them and was condoled with, as far as our ignorance of one another's tongue would allow. Sadly did I stand in need of sympathy. I had come out prepared to face all sorts of perils from real beasts of prey, but to be chased by a commonplace cow was ridiculous as well as unpleasant, and this was a trial for which my mind was not made up. I may here remark, though, that during my sojourn in South America I was never in greater danger from any more romantic animal. The fact is, that the real hardships which one has to encounter in such a life are mostly of a very prosaic character, and yet demand far more resolution and endurance than the sensational adventures one reads about in stories. This will be found to be the moral of my experiences, if they have a moral.

Mine was not to be the only misfortune of the day. There had been a sudden fall of the barometer, and when I came out again, restored by the surgical and sartorial care of the ladies, I found that a strong wind had sprung up, and, to my amazement, saw what looked like a black mountain moving across the plain towards us, while the clear sky was fast thickening with brown-lined clouds.

'A dust storm!' they told me, and almost before I had time to make any further inquiries, it was on us. The air was crowded with birds flying before the fury of the storm. The next indication of its approach was that we felt particles of fine dust blown in our faces; and soon the dust not only increased in denseness, but was mingled with pieces of plants and other substances carried along by the wind with such violence as to make the skin smart when they struck it. The whirling clouds grew larger and thicker, and every one, putting his hand over his mouth, began to make for shelter. A few drops of rain fell which in passing through the dust acquired the consistency of mud; peals of thunder were heard not far off, and before long the force of the wind was so great that it was difficult to keep one's footing.

At the first signs of the storm the cattle grew restless. The *peons* in vain tried to round them up; the great herd surged to and fro, and began to move before the wind. And the last thing we saw, before the dust got so thick that we could see no more, was the whole mass going off at a long, slinging trot.

Most of us were safe in the house by this time, where soon it was as dark as night, and lights had to be brought into the room.

For half an hour or more the darkness continued. To me, there was something almost awful in this strange phenomenon; but the other men seemed to look upon it as a matter of course, and throwing off lightly whatever annoyance they might have felt at this interruption to the day's business, betook themselves to making the best of it, and the dark crowded room was soon a Babel of talk and laughter, while through the din every now and again burst a short, sudden peal of thunder above our heads. But except those few drops the rain did not fall, and the *estancieros* whose camps lay farther on in the track of the storm, were jubilant over the hope that it was being carried away to come down on their ground. Rain is of course most valuable at this time of the year. And when it does rain, it *does* rain on the

Pampas; the weather there knows its own mind, and no mistake about it.

The storm went over as quickly as it had come. The air grew clearer, the light began to reappear, and the thunder was fainter and fainter, as it passed away towards the north-east. All the windows had been closely shut to keep out the dust, and the inside of the house was stifling; so I was glad enough to get out and breathe the pure air, deliciously cool and fresh after the storm. I could see the gigantic cloud of dust sweeping away across the Pampas; the sky above was overcast by broken and shifting clouds, and the wind was still strong. But in two or three hours all around was as calm and clear as in the morning.

These hours, now that the cattle-marking was broken up, I spent in making acquaintance of several countrymen, to whom, as just out from 'home,' I was naturally a very interesting personage. 'How is London getting on?' more than one wanted to know. 'Good crop of fogs and mud this year? Rotten Row the same as ever, eh?'

When so many men, leading such solitary lives as *estancieros* on outlying camps often do, meet together, they have plenty to say to each other, and it was late in the afternoon before the visitors began to go. Our friendly hosts crowned their hospitality by lending me a horse, and between five and six o'clock Desmond and I got off for his station.

But I was destined once more to raise a laugh at my own expense. By the aid of the grammar and dictionary, I essayed to take leave of the lady of the house in proper form, and in her own language. Now, what I ought to have said was: '*A los pies de usted señora,*'—' I lay myself at your feet, my lady;' but by an unlucky blunder, instead of *pies*, I used a word for feet that is only applied to animals, and with a genteel bow politely declared that I laid myself at her ladyship's *patas*,—that is to say, her 'trotters.' No wonder that they laughed!

CHAPTER III.

A RIDE AND A STORY.

WE set off for home, then, and at first I enjoyed the ride very much, and revelled in the delight of galloping over the wide open plain, with not a house or a human creature in sight. One felt as if one drank in life at every breath of this invigorating air, and with all my heart I pitied the poor people I had left behind at home, in their jolting omnibuses and crowded streets. The rain, we found, had fallen heavily in some places. One or two *lagunas* which we passed were filled almost to the edge. The herbage sent out a pleasant smell after the grateful shower. Numbers of foxes and 'such small deer,' drowned out of their holes, were running about ; and here and there sitting sentry at the entrance of one of the *biscacho* burrows which dot all the camp, we caught sight of a grave little grey owl which would stare stupidly at us, and keep twisting its head round and round as if it wished to screw it off. The ground, too, over which we passed, was not so level as most of the country round, but rose and fell in gentle undulations. Several times we saw ostriches and deer not far off, and I, in my exuberance of spirits, started off on a bootless hunt, only to find that I might as well try to chase the wind; for Don Pedro had provided me with a steady, safe, and sober old horse, which had not the least sympathy with my vagaries.

But soon all this was changed. The want of sleep the night before, the excitement, the unaccustomed exercise—for a twenty-mile ride was in these days no everyday matter to me—soon began to tell, and I caught myself asking rather anxiously how far we had yet to go. Then Desmond must needs begin a long account of the country and its institutions, and before we had got half through the list of revolutions and internal dissensions which had so often imperilled the prosperity of the Argentine Confederation, I found my eyes closing in spite of all I could do to keep them open, and had to acknowledge that I was getting terribly tired. But, that my readers may not be in the same predicament, I will here let them have a tale which he told me, as illustrating the state of things in this country, where the settlers, to whom it owes so much of its prosperity, can scarcely conceal their contempt for the character and institutions of the natives—that is, the race formed by the union of the old Spanish colonists and the original inhabitants. It is a tale I heard more than once during my stay, but I will give it as told by my cousin, who was one of the principal actors in the affair.

'When our station was started,' said Desmond, 'both I and my neighbours were troubled by constantly losing things of a kind the least likely to take legs to themselves and walk off. Stealing is unfortunately common enough in this country, but for a time there seemed to be a perfect epidemic of theft in the neighbourhood. Lassos, reins, knives, tools, and things of that sort, were constantly being missed, even from stations where there were no native servants or other suspicious inhabitants. We talked over this state of affairs, and, right or wrong, we were inclined to give the credit of these depredations to a villanous-looking old man who used to hang about under pretence of hunting armadillos, and who was, moreover, suspected of being a *bombero* or spy of the Indians, about the worst character that a man can have among frontier settlements. Some of us had warned this fellow off in no mild terms; but one stormy night he got a lodging at the station of an Englishman called

Darrell. Next morning two of Darrell's dogs were found dead, poisoned in all likelihood, and a revolver was missing. The old armadillo-hunter was missing too, but two or three days later he was heard of as having been at a station on the other side of the town, where he had offered for sale a revolver corresponding to the description of Darrell's.

'This seemed pretty plain evidence, and other bits of proof against the old gentleman turned up, which I need not trouble you by going into: enough to say, that any metropolitan police magistrate would have felt himself justified in sending the case for trial. So Darrell got the Commandante of Villa Grande over to dinner, and asked him to have the suspected man arrested and brought to trial. The Commandante's heart being warmed by *maté* and *caña*, he expressed most friendly sympathy towards the English settlers, and swore that the old armadillo-hunter should be taken forthwith, dead or alive.

'The Commandante was as good as his word. Two or three days afterwards, we heard that the prisoner was safe in the guard-house of Villa Grande, where some of us saw him sitting at the door with heavy irons on his feet, smoking cigarettes, or perhaps shuffling about in front, and begging of the passers-by, or, for want of other sympathizers, chatting in the most friendly way with his ragged guards, who, having probably been criminals themselves, were not disposed to take a very grave view of the offence with which he was charged. Nevertheless, the sergeant, on receiving a couple of dollars from Darrell, was good enough to promise that the fellow should not be allowed to escape; and we thought we might congratulate ourselves that there was now a fair prospect of his being duly brought to justice.

'But justice seemed to be in no hurry to arrive upon the scene. The Commandante, though a few days before he had shot off-hand a couple of soldiers who had tried to desert, refused to take any steps for the punishment of the old man till he had been duly tried by the civil authorities; and to such sound doctrine we Britons could take no exception. When we tried to appeal to the civil power, however, we could get no satisfaction. The *juez-de-paz*, the only magistrate of the town, had gone to Buenos Ayres on political affairs, as we were told, and it appeared to be no one else's business to interfere in the matter. *Quien sabe?* was the only answer to our inquiries when the trial would take place. So the prisoner lay comfortably in the guard-house, and wanted for nothing, being looked upon by his compatriots in the town less as a disreputable member of society than as a martyr to the malice of these detestable *Gringos*, as they called us.

'But Darrell was determined not to let the fellow slip through his fingers; and by dint of writing to the capital of the province, he at last procured that a judge was to be sent down from thence, with authority to hear the case. And sure enough, two or three days afterwards, we were told that the judge had arrived, and those of us who had evidence to give were summoned to appear next day at Villa Grande for the trial.

'We duly appeared at what we thought a proper hour, but were met by the information that as we had not come earlier, the legal official had gone off to see some friends in the camp, and that the trial was adjourned till next morning.

'Very much disgusted, for it was a busy season of the year, all we could do was to make the best of the delay. So I, and one or two others, put up at the *fonda* and passed the time as best we could,—that is, we eat tough steaks and eggs, drank bad coffee, lounged about the town, read some old numbers of an American paper that we routed out somewhere, played billiards on a rickety table, which was more like a hilly country than anything we had seen on the Pampas, and finally went to bed on and under the said billiard table, which served for dining, sleeping, and playing on by turns.

'Next morning the trial did begin, not more than half an hour after the appointed time. It was held in a low, whitewashed edifice, without the least pretence to any of the ceremonial or dignity of the law. The judge, a black-bearded gentleman, with a somewhat dirty shirt and a still dirtier collar, sat behind a table at one end of the room, smoking cigarettes and drinking *maté*; beside him was a boy taking notes. At the other end sat the prisoner, also smoking, guarded by two soldiers, one armed with a very large sword, the other with a rusty blunderbuss. The rest of the court was quite filled up by the witnesses and about half a dozen spectators, who found room where they could, and were occasionally admitted by the judge to the honour of a private conversation on any subject except the matter on hand.

'When the proceedings were about to begin, it was discovered that there was no paper. Accordingly the guard with the blunderbuss was sent to a store to fetch some, and returned with a few sheets of what looked like cigarette paper. The judge then leisurely dictated to his clerk, who, with great deliberation and many flourishes, wrote out something of the nature of an indictment. The other guard was then sent out for some zerba dust to dry the writing with, blotting paper not being used in these parts. The document, thus drawn up, was read over to the prisoner, who replied by a grunt at the end, by way of pleading. I was the first witness. I was invited to take a chair, and opposite me, on a bullock's head, sat the interpreter, a horse dealer of the town, who spoke English rather more badly than I understood Spanish.

'" Are you de parent of de prisoner?" was, to my astonishment, the first question he asked.

'It was *relation* he meant; for, by their law, a criminal's relations cannot give evidence in his case, and this question is always put as a matter of form. But this will serve to show how fit our interpreter was for his work, and to explain how he took more than half an hour to dispose of my evidence, which, after all, amounted to very little. When I had finished, the prisoner was asked if he had anything to ask me; but all he had to say was, "*Es mentira todo!*"—" It's all a lie."

'The other witnesses got disposed of no more speedily. Nobody seemed to take much interest in what was going on, least of all the prisoner, unless it was the judge, who seldom took his cigarette out of his mouth except to make some remark totally unconnected with his functions. Once, when a pretty girl passed by the open door of the court-house, his worship so far roused himself as to get off the bench and run out to look after her; but this was almost the only sign of being awake which he exhibited till soon after midday, when he abruptly broke up the court and went off to take his *siesta*.

'The interval allowed for this and other refreshments was a prolonged one, and it was not till past four o'clock that the sitting was resumed. The droning interpreter was now got rid of, for Darrell himself had arrived on the scene, who could speak Spanish like a native, and did his best to infuse a little spirit into the business. But he found it impossible to stir the slow pace of the trial into even a decent trot; the judge was determined to allow nothing irregular. There were two game-cocks in one corner of the room, which this exalted functionary had been bargaining for; and seeing me looking at them, he coolly stopped the proceedings, while he tried to get up a chat with me on the noble sport of cock-fighting, in which he appeared to be an enthusiast. Then a little more evidence was taken; then the newspaper arrived by the afternoon train, and our judge must have a look at it; then, before long, another interruption for *maté*, and all the while cigarettes and chattering.

'In this way the trial dragged itself along, and as

sunset approached some of us Englishmen grew tired of waiting, especially as the stormy-looking sky warned us to make for home as soon as possible. So I, for one, saddled my horse and rode away with two of my neighbours, saying to ourselves, that let the judge be as slow and stupid as he might, there could be no getting over the plain proofs that had with such deliberation been laid before him, and flattering ourselves that this tiresome job was done, and that the thieving old armadillo-hunter would now come in for his deserts.

'What was our disgust, a few days afterwards, to learn that all these tedious formalities had as yet led to nothing; that the sleepy judge had been sent only to take notes of the evidence with a view to further proceedings, and that as he had no authority to pronounce either verdict or sentence, the criminal was laid up in the guard-house as comfortably as ever!

'"When is he to be tried, then?" we asked of the Commandante, but could get no satisfaction beyond the inevitable "*Quien sabe!*" Our official friend, however, persisted in assuring us that the prisoner was in safe custody, and offered, if we had any doubts, to let a guard of Englishmen keep watch over him. A nice idea, when it was the shearing-time, and most of us were as busy as could be! We refused to take advantage of this offer, but perhaps it put into our heads the notion of giving a shove ourselves to the somewhat heavy wheels of Argentine justice.

'The fact is, there was a good deal of ill feeling between us and the natives at that time; and we could not help suspecting that the armadillo-hunter would get off, if his countrymen could in any way manage it. The priests, who have a good deal of influence in the country districts, had been preaching a sort of crusade against us, provoked by an Englishman who went about giving Bibles and tracts in Spanish to the natives. Then there was an unpleasant affair which didn't help to heal up people's feelings on either side. In these towns there is a rule against riding fast through the streets—why, I don't know. Hearing of this, a foolish young fellow called Price, who had lately come out from Glamorganshire, and on this occasion had probably been making himself too intimately acquainted with the drinks of the country, must needs go galloping through Villa Grande, right past the door of the guard-house. Two of the bare-legged soldiers made a dash at him; his horse stumbled, and one of them caught the bridle and insisted on taking Mr. David Price back to the *fonda*, where it was explained to him that he must pay a fine of a dollar. Price pretended to agree to this, and treated his captors to some *caña*. While they were drinking it, he managed to heat a half dollar piece in the oven, and putting it on the top of another half dollar, presented them to the sergeant of the guard, who was not slow to close his fingers on the money, nor to drop it and run off howling when the hot coin burned his hand. Thereupon Master Price comes off in high glee, and seemed to think he had done something very clever and witty; but I told him he was a fool for his pains, and would hear more than he liked about his joke before he was done with it.

'Sure enough, next day he was summoned to appear before the Commandante, and asked for an explanation of this insult to the officials of the State. The clever youth explained, through the interpreter, that he was sorry if he had done wrong, that he had looked into the law which he was accused of breaking, and was much struck by its clearness and good sense; but that, while a fine was mentioned, it was nowhere said whether the money was to be paid *hot or cold*. The Commandante was not in the least tickled by this pleasantry, but gruffly threatened to have the offender laid up in the guard-house; and the end of it was, that our Welsh friend had to pay for his wit, to a tune which made it clear that native justice was neither blind nor lame, when there was any prey to be caught worth fleecing.

'All this time our indignation had been rising. Another fortnight had gone by, and nothing more had been done in the matter of the armadillo-hunter; and one day, when some seven or eight of us met at a cattle-parting at Darrell's, it was plainly proposed to take the law into our own hands. Some advised a rope and just as much hanging as could be done without killing the fellow; others spoke of a sound thrashing, or a ducking in the *laguna;* anyhow it was agreed to ride to the town that night, pull him out of the guard-house, and give him and the rest of them a lesson that we were not to be trifled with.

'It was a bright moonlight night, and we set off for Villa Grande so as to arrive there about eleven o'clock. We took our revolvers with us in case of accidents, but we did not expect to find much resistance from the native guard. We also took masks of crape or cloth to cover the upper parts of our faces, so that we might not be recognised. Altogether we presented the appearance of a band of highwaymen; but we did not meet a soul on the way to be frightened by us.

'We left our horses just outside of the town, and marched straight for the *cuartel.* We had expected to find the people all in bed at this hour, but unfortunately some *fête* had been going on, and there were lights and sounds of stirring in several of the houses. We met no one, however, as we crossed the *plaza*, and walked up to the guard-house, round the door of which were clustered about half a dozen men, instead of the two or three who usually kept watch there. They were changing the guard, I believe, or perhaps only gossiping; at all events, we didn't suppose it would make much difference having two or three more to deal with, but walked right up to them, taking out our revolvers to show we were in earnest.

'As soon as they saw us coming up in this style they guessed there was something wrong, and raising a yell, disappeared into the inside of the guard-house, barring the door without delay, and forthwith began to shout loudly to us to let them out, as if we were preventing them from displaying their valour.

'We made a rush at the door, and finding it locked, Darrell gave a kick or two to produce silence, then called out that we had come for the prisoner, that we would not hurt any of the others, but that we must have him, and the sooner the better. This was followed up by a few more kicks, by way of intimating that we were in a hurry.

'For a minute or two there was a confused jabbering inside; then the sergeant came to the door, and declared most vehemently that the prisoner was not there.

'"Open the door, or we'll knock the place about your ears," roared Darrell in Spanish. We couldn't help being impatient, for by this time some of the people of the town were coming up to learn what might be the matter.

'There was no answer, and after looking round to see if there was not another way of entrance, we caught up an algaroba post, and using it as a ram, in half a minute or so smashed in the door, and made a charge into the guard-house, catching a glimpse of the man we were in search of, and the guards all huddling together at the other end of the room. That was only for a moment. The first thing which happened was that the lantern was upset; and the whole place plunged in darkness. The next, a blunderbuss went off, as likely as not, by accident, and one of our party was wounded in the shoulder by a slug. Then one or two of us fired our revolvers, and all was confusion, shouting, screaming, swearing, struggling, and uncertainty.

'"Here he is! I've got the scoundrel!" cried one man above the din, and two or three of us dragged the prisoner, as we thought, towards the door. But when we came out into the moonlight, it turned out to be the sergeant's wife in very scanty costume, who screamed and scratched and invoked the saints to much more purpose than she called to her husband to save her from these *brutos*. We let her go fast enough; then it was a question whether it was worth while making a dash into the dark room.

'By this time the people were taking the alarm. Cries of *Los Indios! los Indios!* were heard on every side; at the doors of the houses, and the windows of those that had windows, women were screaming for help; dogs barked, horses neighed; stragglers were hurrying into the *plaza*, and a small crowd had already gathered to watch our proceedings with mingled wonder, perplexity, and fright. Then the broken drum, which served this town instead of an alarm-bell, was sounded, and several other soldiers appeared on the scene, and stood clashing their arms at a respectful distance. We had not expected to raise such a commotion.

'" Have him out! never mind these curs! The whole lot will run at the first shot," cried one or two of the more hot-blooded among us; but there were cooler heads who saw it wouldn't do.

'" We must give it up," said Darrell. " We shall

have a mob upon us in two minutes more, and there will be mischief; so the best thing we can do is to make off at once, before any shooting is wanted."

'Everybody knew that our leader was no coward, and the smallest reflection showed us that a discreet retreat was the better part of valour. Luckily at that moment the moon went behind a cloud, and under cover of the darker side of the *plaza* we drew off, keeping a good front, however, to the mob, who yelled and threw bones and bits of brick, in default of stones, but did not attempt to follow us at first. One or two shots, also, were fired; but as they were aimed at nothing in particular, they had no effect except in increasing the alarm. We got safely out of the *plaza*, and made for the spot where we had tied up our horses, leaving the town behind us in a state of universal uproar.

'A great crowd soon collected round the guardhouse, and by and by arrived the Commandante, very fussy, and very angry to boot, for he had been brought away from a dancing party of the chief people in the town. Among the Babel of tongues he at last got to know something about the cause of the disturbance. Then, after taking some time to reflect, and giving us some time to get off, he set out in pursuit at the head of his regular army of some fifteen men, with a great tag-rag-and-bobtail of excited volunteers.

'Before long they fell in with a boy who offered to guide them to the place where we had taken refuge, which indeed was the tumble-down building that we had put up our horses in, just outside of the town. Cautiously the native forces approached this stronghold, and having surrounded it on every side, proceeded to summon us to come out, lest a terrible fate should befall us. I understand that they remained here for about a quarter of an hour, vowing desperately to slaughter us to a man when they got hold of us. But there was no reply to their threats except the wheezing of an old broken-winded mare which turned out to be the only occupant of the building, when at last they ventured to take it by storm.

'In the meanwhile we were quietly riding home, taking care not to distress our horses, that they might bear no marks of the night's work. We did not expect to be seriously pursued, but we were very much disgusted with ourselves for having taken all this trouble to no purpose; and the boldest of us were obliged to confess that the native authorities would be even more contemptible than we had taken them for, if we didn't hear more about this business. Altogether, when we came to think over it, the affair hadn't been a success.

'But, after all, none of us were called to account for the riot. There was an inquiry, of course, and many conflicting stories were told.

'The tale of the guard was, that they had been suddenly attacked by a large body of Englishmen, who, when they sallied out, had fled at the first shot. Some of the inhabitants, who had not arrived on the scene till all was over, would have it that the Indians were to blame. An old Italian gentleman, much respected in the town, suggested that the guard had been drunk, and had got quarrelling among themselves. No doubt the Commandante had his own opinion on the matter, but considering all things, he thought the less said about it the better. The door of the guard-house was mended, an imposing Argentine flag was stuck up on a pole in front, as a hint to Englishmen and other evil-disposed people that they must mind what they were about; the guard was doubled for the future, and the matter dropped.

'But our exertions seemed not to be altogether thrown away, for soon afterwards the business of the old armadillo-hunter was settled. You have heard of the verdict, "Not guilty, but don't do it again." The finding of the court in this case was very much to the same purpose. The prisoner was acquitted for want of evidence, but was ordered off to the frontier as a disreputable character.'

As I hinted, my cousin's story was, for the time being, mostly thrown away upon me, so sleepy was I. I heard him speaking, but scarcely understood what he was talking about. I knew that the sun had set, and that it was growing dark; as for the horse, it seemed to be marking time, and I had no notion whether it was going forward or not. Once or twice I nearly fell off the saddle, and roused myself with a start for a moment, only to be again overwhelmed by drowsiness. And at last I heard, as in a dream, a great noise of dogs barking, and opened my eyes to find myself in front of a small solitary hut, to which a strapping Briton, who looked big enough to fill up the whole house by himself, was jovially bidding me welcome. This was Bob Eckford, of course. Inside were a candle, and a fire, and a tea-kettle, which, as I dropped, stiff and tired, off my horse, I beheld with sleepy satisfaction.

CHAPTER IV.

LAS BISCACHERAS.

BEHOLD me now an inmate of 'Las Biscacheras;' so the place was called, from the numerous mound-like burrows of these little animals which had been found there. Any one who had seen me leaving England, thin, pale, and languid, would scarcely have recognised me now, already sunburnt, full of spirits, with a tremendous appetite, and eagerly entering into the wild freedom of this new way of life.

Our camp or settlement—I always speak of it as *ours*, for the frankness and friendliness of my hosts was so great, that I soon ceased to look on myself as a guest, and felt so thoroughly at home as to identify myself entirely with their household,—our *estancia*, it must be known, was as yet scarcely a year old, and being situated on the very frontier of the civilised world, as it were, could not pretend to anything like magnificence, was sadly deficient indeed in the comforts which at home would be considered necessary, though at our age and in that glorious climate we did not feel inclined to complain of our accommodation. Now I hear there is a good brick house on the spot, with garden, offices, and even trees, the last not least among the luxuries of such a life. But in those days nothing had been done in the way of building but what was absolutely indispensable. I will try to describe our abode from recollection.

The chief feature was, of course, the dwelling-house, which was nothing more than a small mud hut, its only mark of distinction being a roof of corrugated iron which Desmond had brought from Buenos Ayres in great triumph, but which turned out to be a mistake, inasmuch as it made the place very hot in summer, and very cold in bad weather; at all events, it kept the inside dry. Near the hut was pitched a tent that had been the original abode of the settlers, before they had time to build this more commodious mansion. Besides, we boasted a large and a small *ramada*, which were simply small spaces covered by a reed thatch supported on posts; in the larger of these the saddle-horses were put to stand sometimes, and the smaller was used for hanging up meat and other articles which might be spoilt by the heat of the sun. Behind the *ramadas* had been dug a deep well, out of which water was drawn up in a canvas bag—no easy job, as I ought to know. In the neighbourhood of the well we were trying to make a garden, but not hitherto with much success, though a few melons bore witness that it was intended to be a garden. Behind this was a large patch of young maize. Here and there about the premises stood posts for tying horses to. In front of the house were the *corrals* or yards, a large one fenced with wire for the sheep, and a smaller enclosure of rough and uneven logs for the horses, and for the cattle which in time were to be added, if all went well. So much for the house and offices; then I may truthfully say that we had round us a park of several hundred miles, over which we might look in every direction without seeing a tree, or a house, or a human being, as far as the eye could reach.

The population of this important settlement consisted, at the time of my arrival, of six persons, to wit, Desmond and his partner Bob Eckford, one of the best-natured fellows in the world, Jim their English servant, two native *peons*, dignified and lazy, except on horseback, and a negro boy who bore the high-sounding appellation of Senecio.

The last three lived outside, sleeping, eating, and all in the open air, unless the weather were very unfavourable; Jim's abode was the tent, while we three inhabited the house. Everybody had to work, and the masters worked harder than anybody else. Young gentlemen who can't get on without kid gloves and easy-chairs must on no account come out to the Pampas, where men who once were ornaments of fashionable society find themselves obliged to take a hand in whatever is going, and may often be seen tackling manfully to the most menial employments. Unlikely as it may seem, men of education and refinement are often observed to take more kindly to this unaccustomed life than English working men, who are apt to prove helpless when taken out of their usual rut, and can't make up their minds to do without bacon and beer. Scotchmen and Irishmen are more accommodating, and the frugal Germans and Italians 'come out strong,' as Mark Tapley would say, under circumstances of hardship and privation which make it difficult for John Bull to preserve his jollity.

Of course I was anxious to make myself of use, and after being in the way and lending a hand promiscuously for the first few days, and especially at the well above mentioned, which, as being hard work, yet not requiring skilled labour, was readily handed over to the new-comer, I was at last promoted to the honourable and onerous duty of driving out the flock. Proud of the confidence placed in me, I set off after breakfast on a fresh and somewhat skittish horse, with a Spanish grammar and a copy of Don Quixote in the original in my pocket, wherewith to while away the hours of shepherding. My notions of this pursuit had hitherto been founded on the pictures in old story-books, where an interesting and scantily attired youth is represented as reposing gracefully under the shadow of a spreading beech, and playing on a rustic pipe, while the sheep graze meekly round, or lie peacefully and picturesquely at the feet of their gentle guardian. I had just been reading, too, Don Quixote's enthusiastic descriptions of this innocent and careless state, when he proposed to his faithful squire that they should buy sheep and turn shepherds, and: 'I will complain of absence, thou shalt extol thyself for constancy; the shepherd Carrascon shall complain of disdain; and the priest Curiambo may say or sing whatever he pleaseth, and so we shall go on to our heart's content.' But I soon had less pleasing experiences of a shepherd's life.

At first all went well, with the exception of one harmless tumble which I got as my horse's legs broke through into a *biscacho* hole, an occurrence far from uncommon in riding over the Pampas. But presently, just as I was attempting to commit an irregular verb to memory, my woolly charges began to show signs of unwonted excitement. I was not long puzzled as to the cause; we were in sight of a *laguna*, half dried up, and looking like a shallow muddy pond. As we drew nearer, they could no longer restrain themselves, and a regular stampede took place, the whole flock flying off like so many wild deer, and rushing down in a confused mass upon the water, welcomed as eagerly as if it had been the most limpid stream. I put the grammar in my pocket and rode hard after them. It was useless to attempt to check them; but I was in sore dismay when I saw round the edge the half-buried carcases of animals which had sunk in the soft mud while attempting to reach the water. Luckily the ground in most parts was now baked so dry that it gave a firm passage to the flock; and that anxiety being taken away, it was quite delightful to see the avidity with which the poor things slaked their thirst. My horse, too, put in his claim for a drink; and when the flock had had enough, I dismounted and took the bit out of his mouth—the heavy curb-ring used out there prevents horses from drinking—put the headstall round his neck, and led him down to the edge of the water. But I soon found that the bit made all the difference in my influence over the ungrateful animal. Regardless of my new English boots, he chose the dirtiest place and pushed forward into the mud, which grew softer at every step; and I was obliged to pick my way after him, holding on to the end of the reins, till, to my great satisfaction, he found the water clear enough to drink. An English horse would have stood aghast had such a decoction of black mud and briny liquid, half boiled by the sun, been offered him; but my steed seemed heartily to enjoy the filthy compound, which he sucked up through his close set lips as if through a filter. He gulped and gurgled until I thought he intended to drain out the *laguna* before he stopped, and all the while I was trying to keep myself from sinking over the ankles in the mud. At last he stopped, but it was only to look round on me with a contemptuous chuckle, as I fancied, then to lower his head and begin gulping again. At this point I ventured a gentle pull at the reins, whereupon he stared at me, as if to say, 'Well, what do you want?' Then he began to paw the mud in a playful manner, and another tug made him bolt onwards deeper into the *laguna*. I followed up to my knees, but here the headstall

HORSE PLAY.—*The Pampas*, p. 60.

broke, and the impudent beast, with a frolicsome toss of his heels, treated me to a parting salute of mud and water, and made off to the other bank, leaving me looking like a fool, with the bridle in my hand. They talk about a horse laugh ; I am sure I saw his old sides shaking, and I imagined that he gave me a wink, as, having scrambled out on the other side, he turned round to take a look at his too trustful master.

Wet and muddy, I retraced my steps as best I could, and ran round the end of the *laguna* to catch him, while he moved off slowly as if to provoke me to pursuit. But he had no idea of being caught by such a greenhorn. It was in vain I called out to him, now coaxingly, now in a tone of command or of remonstrance. The perverse brute would stop for a little and graze quietly ; then, just as I was creeping up to him, he would give his head a saucy toss, and be off again to a distance of a couple of hundred yards. I followed him, blown and perspiring, and to my horror perceived that the flock was making off in quite the opposite direction, towards one of their accustomed haunts, while the horse was decoying me farther and farther away from them. I had got altogether confused about the direction in which I had come, and looking round, I could see no sign to guide me homewards. And to make things worse, the mist which had lain lightly on the ground when I started, was now growing thicker, till before long I found myself wrapped in it, and lost sight of the horse altogether, as well as of all other objects. Thicker and thicker it gathered, and here was I all alone in it, with as little notion where to turn as if I had been set down in a pitch-dark night somewhere about the centre of Africa, and told to find my way to Timbuctoo. I walked round and round, seeking vainly for some trace by which to guide my footsteps; then I sat down and tried to wait till the sun should clear away the mist. But the inaction was intolerable, and I struck out again at random, though I did not know but that every step might be leading me farther away from home. At one time I thought I saw my horse, but on coming close it proved to be a gaunt ostrich stalking about, which was off like a shot as soon as it was aware of me. At last, after wandering for, I should think, two hours, I saw some horses looming through the mist. They also made off as I approached, but I followed in the same direction, and soon came upon a dried-up pool which I did not recognise. But going a couple of hundred yards farther, I stumbled upon a sure sign of the neighbourhood of my fellow-men, not a footprint such as astonished the eyes of Robinson Crusoe, but *an empty soda-water bottle.* A few steps more and I heard voices, and at last, to my great relief, found myself close to the house.

Desmond, it seemed, had gone out to look for me, but Eckford was at home, and to him I had to confess my utter failure in taking care of the sheep, and my fears that some woful calamity might be the result of my inexperience.

But he only laughed and took it as a matter of course; and, the mist lifting away, we presently rode out together, and were not long of hitting upon the truant flock, while my runaway horse was discovered among his companions grazing as comfortably as if he had nothing to be ashamed of. Fortunately the sheep had taken a direction in which they might range for probably hundreds of miles without meeting any other flock to get mixed with; in the more thickly stocked camps, such a going astray might have become a serious matter.

After all, the only injury done was to my saddle. The unprincipled horse, by way of celebrating his independence, had amused himself by rolling on the top of it, and it was rubbed and scratched in a manner to shock the eminent Piccadilly saddler from whose faultless establishment it had been sent out not twelve months before.

Before leaving the colony I had acquired experience enough not to let myself be made a fool of by the sheep; I had also learned the unsoundness of the popular view as to the moral and sentimental character of these animals, whom I now deliberately affirm to be a race of woolly humbugs. They are very pretty and interesting objects when you see them from the railway, frisking or dozing in the meadows; but when you have had much to do with them in the way of business, you will find that there is no more tiresome and disagreeable creature than your innocent, baaing, docile-looking sheep. And these much praised lambs are the worst of all for stupidity and perverseness! Their most provoking trick is falling behind the rest of the flock, and going to sleep, when, if you don't look after them, they are pounced on as a dainty morsel by the hungry vultures that are always hovering about over the Pampas. They have a way out there of coming into the world at all times of the year; but at the chief lambing season, the shepherd's life becomes almost unbearable. What with mammas that have lost their children, children that don't know their mammas when they see them, and aunts and grandmothers who insist on adopting unwilling youngsters, the most respectable flock is turned into a perfect Babel of bleating and confusion, and it requires the fabulous patience so unjustly attributed to sheep, for the shepherd to get all to rights. Then their proneness to follow bad example is only equalled by their utter inability even to understand good advice; and on the whole, their conduct is such that I am astonished they should continue to be held up as models to young gentlemen and ladies, who may at least be reasoned with, and persuaded, if the arguments used be strong enough.

But in the meanwhile I was temporarily released from pastoral cares. Such intimate and constant acquaintance with the saddle as is usual in camp, produces in most new-comers an unfortunate crop of boils which for a time puts horse exercise out of the question. I was not exempted from this ordeal; and during its continuance, that my valuable services might not be lost to the community, I was permitted to exchange into the cookery department, in which I flatter myself that I displayed some innate talent.

On the first day of my performance in this capacity, I rose early and began operations by bringing in firewood. In my zeal, I lighted the fire before considering what was to be cooked on it, and on making inquiries, found that our intended breakfast was feeding unsuspiciously about a mile off. Fortunately yesterday's joint was still partly available, and I cut the remains of it into slices, or rather junks, and brandered them in a style which was pronounced excellent by my hungry friends. Dinner was a more serious affair, but in the meanwhile Jim had caught and killed the mutton for me, and I addressed myself boldly to my task. Determined to aim at distinction as a cook, I scorned the usual *asado*, or roast done on a spit, and set my mind upon a savoury mess such as should recall the luxuries of home. I cut off a good piece of the ribs and put it in a pot. Next I got some rice, but was puzzled to know the proper quantity to put in; however, I made a guess at it, and committed the mess to the flames, adding some pieces of pumpkin, and after nearly an hour and a half's boiling, was delighted to find the result a splendid success. The meat was rather tough, indeed, from having been boiled too fast, but in the camp one has generally good teeth. This was not all; I hit upon the grand idea of stewing kidneys, which were generally thrown away there. I got the kidneys of the sheep killed in the morning; these I left stewing beautifully, while I went to the tent for some tea —we took tea with all our meals. On my return I found that the stew had taken advantage of my absence to behave in an extraordinary manner. The water had risen up in one great yellow bubble as high again as the pan. I feared the whole mess was going to fly up the chimney, and made a dash at the rebellious kidneys, but *whew!*—of course I burned my fingers. My only other difficulty was with the flour, which, instead of thickening the gravy as it should have done, persisted in running into little lumps. After all, though, the kidneys were capital, and I ran some risk of being employed in cooking all the time of my stay.

We all took our turn at this work, and I may say that by the aid of a little practice and some study of the subject in *Chambers's Information for the People*, I became quite an adept in the culinary art. Jim was by far our best cook, however; though, unfortunately, he was not so fastidious about means and materials as was to be desired, and we were at great pains to persuade him that moderately clean hands were among the necessities of this office. One day, in our absence, he contrived for us the unusual treat of fried steaks, and it was only when we had eaten heartily of them, that somebody thought of asking him where he had got the grease.

'Where? why, I took one of the tallow candles,' he replied, to my horror.

In the peaceful occupation of cooking, I had one narrow escape from an accident which may seem too good to be true. In that part of the country, where there are so few trees, every scrap of wood is of value. To make posts, we had carted down from Villa Grande an *algaroba*-tree with a large, stumpy root, which latter was by no means to be wasted. So Bob Eckford, after hacking at it for some time with a blunt axe, thought the quickest way of splitting it would be to drill a hole and blow it up with gunpowder. But the fuse would not go off, and being called away to the *corral*, he left the job to be done another time. Presently I arrived upon the scene with my pot, and seeing the stump lying handy, I thought it was just the thing to make a good blaze. So, having lit the fire,—I don't know if I mentioned that in hot weather we generally made our fire out of doors,—I arranged the stump nicely on it, piled up chips round about, and set the pot on the top of all. At this juncture Eckford happened to stroll up, and, as soon as he saw what I was doing, he began to yell in a manner so unlike his usually placid and easy-going disposition, that I thought he must have gone mad. My astonishment increased as he rushed forward, reached the fire in a dozen long strides, and vigorously kicked it over, pot and all. It was only when he had the charred stump safe in his arms, that he explained to me how in a few minutes more our dinner would most likely have been blown up—and myself into the bargain!

Though we were our own cooks, you are not to understand that we were altogether without pretensions to gentility. We had a flunkey to wait on us at dinner, Senecio to wit, a fat, curly-headed, black boy, who, not to put too fine a point upon it, had been *given* to Eckford by his mother. Though he chiefly confined his exertions to showing his teeth and putting his elbows in the dishes, he always, for the look of the thing, stood behind us at meals, dressed in a dirty pair of white cotton gloves, and in very little else, for which reason, on the *lucus a non lucendo* principle, he was also addressed as 'Buttons' while performing this function. Senecio's strong point was his good-nature, which was proof against anything. Rather too much so; for though, when he was scolded, he would try to look preternaturally solemn, there was always a twinkle in his eye, and a moment afterwards he would be in his usual state of broad grin again. His weak point was laziness; or, regarding him in the light of an intimate attendant, I might say it was dirtiness, a failing in which he was by no means singular in this country. In very hot weather we had sometimes to dispense with his services altogether in the confined space of our little hut, and even in the open air his proximity was not felt to be always agreeable. We remonstrated with him, and for a time Senecio pleased us by displaying great zeal for ablution. Every day he came to ask permission to go down to bathe in the *laguna;* and though the water here was not more than a foot deep, we hailed this as a step in the right direction, and our page was allowed to absent himself for two hours daily. But as, after several of these visits, he only seemed to have become more dirty than ever, we kept a closer eye on his proceedings, and discovered that the greedy little rascal's sole employment at the *laguna* was eating a kind of sour plum called *chanar*, which grew on a few bushes by the waterside. Whereupon Eckford chastised him with a strap till poor Senecio repented copiously, and promised to wash every day for the gratification of the *patron*. But to make sure, we took him down to the water on Saturday night, and superintended a vigorous scrubbing, the result of which was that he came out of the water quite a changed creature. He looked as if he had shrunk up, and become smaller, having left a considerable portion of himself in the *laguna*.

In my study of Spanish I made great use of Senecio, at first to practise upon; but I soon found it impossible to judge of my success in trying to speak the language, inasmuch as Senecio always grinned at whatever was said to him, whether he understood it or no. He never could or would learn English, beyond the few words which he could not help picking up from us; but he had a quick ear for music, and it was one of Eckford's amusements to teach him popular songs, the choruses of which he used to bellow lustily, excelling, as might be supposed, in those melodies which are chiefly made up of a noisy and nonsensical refrain. His performance of 'Hoop de dooden doo' was equal to that of any London street boy. On the morning after my arrival, I was awakened by a song which seemed somehow familiar to me, though I could not at first catch the words. I soon discovered that Senecio, as he rubbed the mud from our boots, was attempting our national melody—

> 'Rule, Britannia! Britannia rules the waves!
> Britons never, never, never shall be slaves.'

I like to recall all these little features of this life on the Pampas, into which I entered with such zest, but I fear the reader may think I have made a dull chapter of it. If he will have patience with me, I believe I can promise him a little excitement before long.

CHAPTER V.

UNWELCOME GUESTS.

THE things which I had brought out from England, and which Desmond's agent had undertaken to send on, seemed a long time in arriving. The proceedings of custom-houses and goods trains are not rapid in any part of the world, and are peculiarly slow in the Argentine Republic. My friends began to get impatient, for they were sorely in need of some new clothes, shirts and stockings especially; and I was little less desirous that they should have their supplies, inasmuch as, for the meantime, they borrowed freely from my small stock. Then there were a stove, a lamp, and a camp-bed, blankets, and other useful articles; a rifle, a set of garden implements, and a parcel of seeds; a good tool-box for Eckford, and a medicine-chest for Desmond, who had at one time been a medical student, and was still given to dabbling in drugs,—an accomplishment which on the Pampas might at times be very useful, and perhaps again very much the reverse, when there was no other doctor at hand to correct any blunders which a somewhat inexperienced one might make.

At the beginning of December, however, we heard that they had arrived at Villa Grande, but we could not send over for them at once, as the shearing was going on—the most important event of the year.

About twenty natives were hired for this work, and it was a busy time for all. The sheep being driven into the *corral*, they were caught and dragged into a shed, where the shearers operated upon them more quickly than might have been expected. The fact is, they were paid by the fleece; and to me was assigned the duty of rushing about with a bag of tin counters, and giving out one for every fleece rolled up and laid aside. The fellows tried to cheat me, not only by leaving the wool on the sheep's bellies, but by making one fleece into two; and I had to be very sharp, and to learn to look out for the tail in each case. Once, though, I made a great mess by letting my bag fall, so that a heap of counters rolled out on the ground. With a great show of politeness and zeal, my *gaucho* friends scrambled about for them, and pretended to give me back all they could pick up, but I fear my hosts were losers by this piece of awkwardness.

Though the days were so hot, the nights were sometimes frosty, and many of the shorn lambs died. We had no accommodation for the shearers, who had to sleep on the ground as best they could, wrapped in their *ponchos*. In the evening, when their work was over, they used to gather together and amuse themselves by singing and dancing to the music of a guitar, or listening to an extemporary duet between two of their number, who were celebrated for proficiency in this accomplishment, and seemed to give great satisfaction to the audience, though to me their strains sounded doleful in the extreme, and like nothing so much as two cats *miauing* at each other. A painter would have found a striking subject in one of these performances. The seriousness and attention of the audience, their dark faces half revealed by the firelight, their motionless attitude as they sat, or rather squatted on the ground, their variegated dress, and the grave, deliberate way in which they smoked their cigarettes or sipped their *maté*, all struck me as very picturesque, or, at all events, thoroughly un-English.

Occasionally they would treat us to a serenade, in which the virtues of one and the other *patron* were alternately extolled in an exaggerated style, which, if we had understood all they were saying, ought to have made us blush. But of course the motive spring of these performances was not so much their overpowering veneration for us, as the hope of getting a little gin and tobacco. This was what Bob Eckford used to call *ginuine* admiration, and certainly at a very small expense we had as much of it as any Homeric hero could expect.

The shearing was over in about a week, and on the very first day he could, Desmond went to Villa Grande to fetch the things, taking with him all the men and two carts, one our own, and one borrowed from the Simpsons, two brothers who had a station some miles off. Bob Eckford and I were left behind to take care of the place.

After a good morning's work at the fencing of the *corral*, which some of the *gauchos* had been tampering with in the interest of their fire, we treated ourselves to a *siesta*, from which we awoke, as usual, feeling very tired and relaxed, 'like a wet towel hung over the back of a chair,' as an American acquaintance of ours used to say. Driving out the sheep, and leaving them for once to take care of themselves, we did not feel at all inclined for any further exertion, and thinking we had done enough for one day, agreed to indulge ourselves in an early dinner, it being now about four o'clock; for, to suit the travellers, we had breakfasted earlier than usual, and it being moonlight, they would probably not come back till late. I must not forget to mention Senecio, who also formed part of our garrison, but had been in disgrace all day in consequence of a suspicion—only, I fear, too well founded—of helping himself out of the jar of *arrope*, a kind of syrup made from the *algaroba* bean, and from water-melons, which we used to eat with our biscuits, and which, if not kept out of Senecio's way, was generally too strong a temptation for his honesty.

So here we are, sitting in our dining-room, drawing-room, bed-room, and kitchen, a magnificent apartment of sixteen feet by twelve, with two narrow slits which answer the double purpose of lighting and ventilation. Through the open door we see nothing but grass, grass, stretching away till the eye of the gazer fails him. The floor is covered with a carpet of grass trodden bare in several places, so as to give the appearance of a pattern; and the rough walls are ornamented with a plate of Paris fashions from some illustrated newspaper, and with two well-thumbed valentines from home. A great part of the room is taken up by our table, which has a covering indeed, but of grease, though we boast an unusually plentiful supply of plate—to wit, three tin mugs, two cracked willow-pattern plates, one spoon, and a teapot that has seen better days. Our knives we always carry with us, *gaucho* fashion, and put to all uses.

The occupants are variously employed. Bob Eckford, reclining in a corner, is playing on a concertina, and teaching Senecio to dance a reel,—an exercise into which that light-hearted youth enters with great gusto, his black skin seeming to shine more brightly, and his thick hair to stand up more stubbornly than ever, as he capers about and grins, and evidently has quite dismissed from his mind the peccadillo of the morning. Your humble servant, in his shirt and trousers, is removing from the fire a piece of *asado*, or ribs of mutton roasted on a spit, which, with tea and biscuit, is to form our meal. Two dogs sit by, gravely but anxiously eyeing these preparations, and only now and then turning their heads to cast a look of stolid surprise at Senecio's antics.

Suddenly there is an interruption to this peaceful scene. As I place the meat on the table, and am dressing for dinner by rolling down my shirt sleeves an ill-conditioned cur belonging to one of the *peons,* makes a dash through the door, leaps on the table, seizes the mutton, spit and all, and is off with it to the boundless plain.

'*Caramba!*' screams Senecio, snatching up the stob of wood which serves us for a poker, and away we all, dogs and men, rush in pursuit, barking, shouting, and vowing vengeance against the impudent intruder, which has thus robbed us of our dinner. Bob Eckford and I fired several shots from our revolvers, and, more by good luck than good aim, the fugitive is hit, drops his prey, and rolls over on the grass. But before we can recover our dinner, Senecio sets up a new and louder howl, and, grasping Eckford by the arm, points to the south, and exclaims—

'*Los Indios! los Indios! somos muertos!*'

We turn and look. Sure enough, a large body of mounted men are riding rapidly towards us; and before I can fully realize what has happened, Eckford has dragged me back into the hut, and we are hastily barricading the door, while Senecio coils himself up in the corner and utters doleful cries, till Bob, standing over him with the before-mentioned wooden poker, insists forcibly on his holding his tongue and not betraying the weakness of our garrison.

It all seemed to have passed in a moment, and somehow I took it more as a matter of course than might have been supposed, that I was at last about to encounter the Indians, of whom I had read with so warm excitement in my schoolboy days. We had, of course, discussed the probability of such an attack; but when Butler and Eckford bought the land, they were assured that the Indians had not been seen in the district for years; and their fear of fire-arms was said to be so great, that Englishmen had got into the way of speaking contemptuously of them.

'If they had only come to-morrow!' exclaimed Eckford, looking ruefully at his half-empty revolver.

Indeed, they could not have chosen a worse day for the attack. We had fire-arms indeed, but our ammunition was almost exhausted. To get a fresh supply was the chief reason why Desmond had lost no more time in going to Villa Grande; and now, besieged in this frail hut, we had only five cartridges between us in our revolvers, besides an unloaded horse-pistol, which we capped and served out to Senecio, giving him strict instructions not to pull the trigger, but to make as much of it in the way of display as he could. When we came to reflect on it, our position was indeed serious, and we bitterly regretted the shots we had thrown away on that thievish cur. But we had no time for regrets; we had scarcely finished our preparations before the Indians were round the hut, shouting like demons and beating on the roof with their lances. I won't deny that my heart beat less steadily than usual, as I heard these sounds, and could not keep out of my mind the many tales that were told in the camp of these savages, whose cruelty was said to be equal to their cowardice. But, outwardly at least, I did not lower our national reputation for courage in the eyes of Senecio ; and Eckford set me a splendid example of coolness, though, no doubt, he saw our danger more clearly than I did.

'Shall I fire?' I asked eagerly.

'Don't be a fool,' was his reply. 'We haven't a shot to fire away, man.' Then, calling out in Spanish, he asked what the Indians wanted.

We posted ourselves each at one of the slits on either side of the door; and the *cacique* or chief came close up to the hut, and spoke in Spanish, which he appeared to understand pretty well. Eckford translated as much as was necessary into English, for my benefit; and while this communication was going on, I had time to take a good look at some of our unwelcome visitors. They were short, active fellows, with copper-coloured skins, low necks, smooth faces, and long straight hair. Such dress as they wore consisted mainly of bits of dirty sheepskin, with here and there a more pretentious garment, that no doubt had been dishonestly come by. Round their heads was tied a dirty cloth, that might have been called a turban, if it had not been more like a dishclout. The most villanous-looking of the party were one or two men, whom we took to be runaway *gauchos*. All were well mounted and armed with *boleaderos*, knives, and lances about eighteen feet long, most of the latter ornamented towards the point with a bunch of ostrich or other feathers. These they waved in the air, at the same time making a peculiar noise by screaming, and putting their fingers on their lips, as if playing a diabolic flute. But they all became silent when the *cacique* began to speak. He was decidedly superior to the rest in equipment. He wore a battered felt hat, and a striped *poncho*, and had a large sword by his side, as well as a rusty old pistol, which, however, seemed to want the lock. While conversing with us, he stuck his spear in the ground as a sign of friendship. Throughout the interview we were struck by a certain air of dignity with which he transacted his questionable business; and evidently the rest were completely under his orders.

He began by informing us that he had come to pay us a friendly visit. We did not say that we were glad to see him, but Bob Eckford went straight to the point, and bluntly asked him what they wished to get out of us, at the same time taking care to make a little show of his revolver. To this the *cacique* replied that he should be very glad of anything we could give him ; whereupon Bob handed out a waistcoat, a lasso, and some tobacco, and said that we could spare nothing more. This only whetted the cupidity of the *cacique*, who intimated that his men expected a present all round, and suggested that he should come inside and choose for himself; but we thought that we could understand each other much better so long as he stayed where he was. His next proposal was that we should give up Senecio, as the band was in want of a boy to cook for them. This we also refused, though Senecio, on hearing himself mentioned, took to howling again with such vigour, that Bob told him he had a good mind to take this chance of getting rid of him. When he found that his polite insinuations were all thrown away, the chief raised his voice, and threatened that the house should be brought about our ears if we did not open the door at once.

All the time we had been considering our situation, and now we agreed that our likelihood of making a successful defence was extremely small. It was a great mistake to have left no openings in the walls but these narrow slits, through which we could fire with only a chance of hitting one or two of our assailants, and would then, with empty barrels, have to deal with the rest, infuriated by the loss of their comrades. Our iron roof, too, of which Desmond had been so proud, was seen to be a most doubtful protection; for nothing would be easier than for the Indians to leap on it, strip off one or two of the sheets of metal, and reach us with their long lances, without exposing themselves. We were boxed up in a trap, and saw now, when too late, the mistake we had made in leaving the open for this worse than useless shelter. What was to be done?

'*Somos muertos! somos muertos!*' Senecio began again, doing his best to shake our nerves in such an emergency.

There was short time for taking counsel. The Indians were growing impatient, and began to poke into the hut the heads of their spears, red with the blood of one of our poor dogs, and to point to the things which they wanted, and could see hanging on the walls. Already they were at work to break down the house, and we could feel it shaking as one man dealt tremendous blows with an axe upon the frail walls. The best thing we could do was to make a rush out, and I was promising myself to sell my life as dearly as I could, when my companion called out that he had a proposal to make to the chief, and hurriedly whispered to me what, in his opinion, was our only chance of safety.

The *cacique* at once made his men draw back, and Eckford told him that we were willing to come out into the *corral*, with our arms in our hands, and that, if the Indians promised not to harm us, they might have their will of the house. To these terms the *cacique* willingly agreed, and, after seeing his men drawn up in a line some little way back, and warning him that we would fire at the least appearance of treachery, we threw open the door, and stood face to face with our enemies.

To our surprise, we found that the party did not consist of more than twenty or thirty men, who had among them perhaps as many unmounted horses, which at a little distance had made the numbers of the party appear much greater. We took courage at this; but Eckford would not move a step forward till the nearest of our friends had removed themselves rather farther off, so little did he trust the chief's protestations of good faith. All was done as we desired, and forth we marched into the *corral*, with our revolver in our hands, I being in addition armed with the poker above mentioned, and Bob Eckford carrying under his arm his beloved concertina, from which he was resolved never to part.

As soon as we had reached the point stipulated

upon, the Indians broke loose, and flinging themselves from their horses, rushed pell-mell into our little habitation. The *cacique*, however, seemed determined that the work of plundering should be done systematically, for he ordered them all out but two or three, with whose assistance he proceeded to pick out whatever he thought might be of use to them.

'" Can't be cured, must be endured!"' muttered Bob, trying to take as philosophical a view of the matter as he could.

It was a new sensation to both of us, this of standing by and seeing our property stolen before our eyes; but to tell the truth, we were not very much concerned, as there was little in the hut of any value, and new supplies of everything were coming from Villa Grande. A few minutes before, we had known what it was to feel in danger of our lives; and now that the Indians were seen to pay decided respect to our revolvers, not knowing the state of our ammunition, our spirits rose, and we were even in a mood to enjoy the ludicrous aspects of the scene. These were not wanting. It was amusing to see the grave wonder with which one of the fellows inspected our venerable teapot, and after turning it round on all sides, put the spout to his mouth and took a long suck, but did not seem to approve of the flavour, for he threw it down and entered the hut.

When he came out, he brought our pictorial sheet of the fashions, which he stuck on the point of his lance, and carried away like a standard won from the enemy. The dirtiest of them all was much impressed by the look of our only clean towel, which he tried to fold round his waist, evidently taking it for an article of holiday costume. Another was triumphantly exhibiting a bottle, which he no doubt supposed to contain *caña*, or some other strong liquor; but we fairly roared with laughter at the eagerness with which he secured this prize, for it was half full of nothing but castor oil, provided by Desmond as a panacea in all cases of disease, and we heartily hoped that the new possessor would lose no time in taking a good swig at it. But Bob's laughter was changed to disgust when he saw that the chief had appropriated a pair of patent leather boots, almost his only remaining piece of European finery, and the envy of all our countrymen for twenty miles round. 'One comfort is, they will give him corns,' he growled out to me, as the *cacique* fitted them on to his naked feet. Beyond these things, an old hat, a shirt or two, and a bag of nails which they found in the tent, there was nothing which our visitors seemed to fancy; and in a few minutes they mounted and prepared for a move.

We, you may be sure, kept a very sharp look-out

on them at this point; but they did not attempt to come nearer us. Only the chief rode up to the fence of the *corral*, and assured us that he did not mean any harm to us, and trusted we should henceforth be the best of friends. To this Bob Eckford replied, in the same strain, saying he hoped the boots would fit, and that he should be extremely glad to meet his new friend again at the Old Bailey. The *cacique* called out *hasta luego*, which is the Spanish for *au revoir*, and the whole party, with a chorus of parting yells, began to ride away, while Bob, entering into the fun of the thing, struck up 'The Rogue's March' on his concertina.

But above all the noise rose a familiar cry, and we saw poor Senecio being carried away on the saddle-bow of one of the Indians. He had been afraid to come out of the hut, and in our excitement we had not thought of him till now. Glad as we were to see the backs of our visitors, we were much concerned at the fate of the poor little fellow, who had often caused us so much amusement, and at that moment both of us would have given a good deal for the help of half-a-dozen well-mounted and armed Englishmen. But what could we do? Our two rifles were away with the rest of the party; we could only look on helplessly, till we could no longer distinguish Senecio among the crowd of dusky forms. And we did not yet know the worst.

We got on the roof of the hut to watch the Indians, who rode for some distance at full gallop towards the quarter from which they came. Suddenly they wheeled to the right, and running our eyes along their new line of march, we saw our little troop of horses quietly feeding. We were not long left in doubt as to the intentions of our *friends*. They 'rounded up' the horses, and once more turning to the south, were soon out of sight with the whole troop; luckily the best of them were away with Desmond.

This was too much of a joke, and now that the fun and excitement of the affair was over, we felt extremely disgusted, as we set to work putting things right inside the hut, and speculated how our companions would receive the bad news which we had to give them on their return. Our fear now was that they, too, would fall in with another party of the Indians; and when we had done all we could towards restoring the dwelling to its wonted appearance, we spent an anxious hour or two in watching the road to Villa Grande.

Towards sunset we saw the carts making their way across the camp, and were relieved to find that Desmond and his convoy had seen nothing of the

Indians. But you may imagine their wrath when they heard what had happened in their absence. The two *peons*, indeed, only shrugged their shoulders and said *Caramba!* It was no great business of theirs. Probably they were rather pleased than otherwise to have been out of the way of fighting; and, like the rest of the *gauchos*, they were accustomed to preserve on all occasions a stolid imperturbability of manner. But Jim, our English servant, professed himself much disappointed to have lost such a chance of displaying his valour; and Desmond, who had not such an easy temper as his partner, used very strong language, and vowed that the next time we had such visitors, they should not go away so easily.

All we could do, however, was to make the best of it; and when we saw our new furniture and the box of clothes which I had brought from an outfitter's in London, we agreed our losses were not so much to be regretted,—except, of course, the horses, and Senecio. So we sat down to supper in a tolerably cheerful frame of mind, though every now and then Desmond would growl out a remark about the *cacique*, which that dignitary would scarce have cared to hear, unless he had a good many miles of camp between himself and the speaker.

The rest of the evening was spent by Bob and

me in bewailing the lost Senecio, whose good qualities we now readily called to mind, while we were willing to forget his faults. Desmond, for his part, employed himself in drawing up a memorial to the authorities, very much after the style of the indignant paterfamilias who writes to the *Times* about perambulators or barrel-organs, calling on them to prevent and punish such depredations. I will here mention that the letter was sent, but never answered.

Just as we were preparing to retire to rest, we were startled by hearing the trampling of a horse. We all rushed to the doorway, and by the moonlight saw that the horse had a rider, who in reply to our challenge shouted out—

'Oh, Kafoozlem! Kafoozlem! Kafoozlem!'

'Senecio!' we exclaimed with one voice; and it was our black boy, and no other, who jumped from the horse and ran among us, showing lively signs of joy and affection.

By the light of the new paraffin lamp, which was now the chief ornament of our abode, we saw that Senecio was not much the worse of his short captivity; and we were all eager to know how he had managed to escape. He told us that the Indians had taken him about a hundred miles south—this was of course a tremendous exaggeration on Master Senecio's part; but telling the truth was never one of his strong points. They had stopped for the night by the banks of a river, and Senecio finding himself unobserved for a moment, had contrived to get on the back of one of our best horses, and made a bolt for it. We were astonished at the unexpected boldness which he represented himself as having displayed, but no doubt the cunning little rogue had not failed to notice that the Indians' horses were tired out by a long day's journey. At all events, he got clear off, and giving the horse his head, the animal's unerring instinct took him straight home at full gallop.

The little he had seen of the Indians did not seem to have disposed him favourably towards them; for he now flatly refused to sleep as usual in the tent with the *peons*, for fear of being again carried off. Out of consideration for the adventures he had just passed through, we allowed him to lie down by the fire, after keeping up his spirits by a good supper, and showing him that our arms were all loaded and ready. Of course we knew that there was little chance of the Indians returning so soon; but the worst was, that having been so successful in their first foray, they probably would come back again, some time or other. So Desmond and his partner were not without subject for anxious thought when they lay down that night.

We were to see more of *Los Indios* before I left the country, and luckily were to meet them under more satisfactory conditions. Since then, I have made the acquaintance of the peaceable red men of the Canadian lakes. But even now, when I have the nightmare, I sometimes start up to find myself troubled with a vague terror that the Indians are upon us, and that our last cartridge is gone, and am thankful to find it is only a dream, and to hear the steady footfall of the policeman on his beat outside. I fear some of my youthful adventurous readers may despise me; but the plain truth is, that I have no taste for deeds of violence, and care neither for killing nor being killed. 'Live and let live' is my motto, but it is not always easy to carry out this principle on the frontier settlements of the Pampas.

CHAPTER VI.

A JOURNEY UP THE COUNTRY.

WE lost no time in making preparations against another possible visit of the Indians. As soon as they found themselves in a position to build a regular house, Desmond and Eckford were resolved to construct it for defence, according to the most approved principles of camp-engineering; in the meanwhile, all they could do was to knock some more loopholes in the walls of the hut. In the ground, to secure us against any failure of ammunition, we buried a tin biscuit-box full of cartridges, without mentioning the fact to our faithful *peons*, whom we suspected, perhaps unjustly, of having more friendly relations with the Indians than might be considered desirable. These gentlemen, much to their disgust, we set to work digging a ditch round our camp; a precaution which Desmond had been advised to take at the first, for the horses in this country can't jump. And you may be sure we took care to keep a good look-out in the direction of the *tierra adentra* from which these marauders might be expected to come.

Three of our horses came back to us on the evening after they had been taken away, with their manes and tails cut, and sores on their backs, produced by the bad saddles of the Indians. In this country the horses show a singular attachment to the place where they have been brought up, the *querencia*, as it is called, and also to the companions with which they are accustomed to feed. It is usual to keep them in *tropillas* of about a dozen, led by a bell-mare, or *madrina*, whom they follow wherever she leads, and do not seem content even to eat unless they are near her. When a horse that has been on duty is unsaddled and let loose, he first takes a hearty roll on his back, then, after a good sniff in the air, makes straight for his *tropilla*, though they may be a mile or two away. I have seen one which had been hard at work all day without touching a blade of grass, refuse to go to pasture because his *tropilla* was shut up, and there he stood, snuffing sorrowfully at the posts of the *corral* as long as I watched him. *Tropillas* are formed by collaring each young horse for a time to the *madrina;* but to accustom a *tropilla* to a new camp, as, for instance, when an *estancia* is started, is by no means an easy matter, and takes time and care. It can only be done by putting *mancas* (hobbles) on the mare, shutting the whole of the animals up during the night, when they are most prone to wander, and constantly watching them by day. A horse thus attached to any particular locality is said to be *querenciado;* and this trait in their character is sometimes very inconvenient, as in the case of buying, and sometimes very useful to the owners, when stealing is in question. It is a comfort to know that, if a good horse be stolen from you, the thieves must keep sharp watch over him, or he will take the first chance of coming straight back. It is also a convenience to be able to ride a horse fifty miles, take the bridle and saddle off him, give him a gentle hint in the rear, and make sure that he will turn up at home without stopping to play at marbles on the way, like an idle errand-boy. Some horses show this characteristic much more than others, being known as *muy volvedores;* such animals are almost useless anywhere but at home, as they will leave a new owner, even when years have passed since the transference. I have heard of a fine horse travelling in this way, from the far north of

Paraguay to the province of Entre Rios, which must be nearly seven hundred miles, I should think.

But we saw nothing more of the rest of our animals, and though Christmas was coming on, and we had resolved to spend it in becoming mirth and ease, it was necessary to look about for a reinforcement in this department.

A few days before Christmas, we heard that a party of Indians had sold some horses to a native *estanciero*, near a place called Riados, a good way up the country. Christmas time or not, it seemed desirable that somebody should go to see into the truth of the story, and to get back our missing steeds by purchase, or by the uncertain operations of justice; and it was arranged that Eckford should start at once. I was very glad to accompany him, and Jim our English servant was to be of the party.

I have not hitherto said much about Jim,— Swivel-eyed Jim, as he was generally called,—who was nevertheless a great character. He was a sallow, skinny, squinting little fellow, of varied and, it may be said, doubtful antecedents, but by no means the least useful man about the place, for he could turn his hand to anything, and knew the ways of the country like a native. Out there, Jim was a perfect treasure; at home he would not have been thought so much of. For one thing, he was horribly dirty; and even more careless than the rest of us about his personal appearance, which is saying a good deal. The principal part of his ordinary costume was a coat made of an old sack, which had been so hardened by time and grease, that he used to rub his knife on the sleeves when he wanted to put a fine edge on it. On very high days and holidays, he would put on a clean collar and a long Spanish knife; and when he was got up in this way, there was no speaking to him, for he seemed to think that the extraordinary trouble he had taken entitled him to give himself all the airs of a dandy. As a rule, however, dress was certainly not Jim's weakness; it was rather eating. I never saw such a fellow to guzzle. He would stow away twice as much as the biggest man on the station, but only looked all the leaner for it. The one objection he had to South America was that, living upon beef and biscuit for weeks together, as we often had to do, he was deprived of the flesh-pots of his youth; and I remember he was especially eloquent about the charms of a *squab-pie*, a luxury of his native Devonshire, which he assured us was well worth going home for. Whenever he was in a grumbling mood, he would give out that this attraction was too strong for him, and that he must return to the land of squab-pies; but as he never could keep his money, he was obliged to stay where he was, and content himself with devising the most remarkable messes for his own behoof. This was just as well for Desmond and Eckford; inexperienced as they were, I don't know how they could have spared him in the infancy of their settlement. He was clearly the man to go with us on such important business.

Well, we three started, and made a safe but uninteresting and unsuccessful journey to Riados. We put up there for a day at the *fonda,* or small inn, where we slept on tables in a room full of tobacco smoke and other more unmentionable inconveniences. There were only two rooms, so it was just as well that we had the whole house to ourselves, few visitors ever requiring accommodation at this out-of-the-way place, except on the one night in the week when the diligence passed through.

The town, or village, was simply a collection of mud houses, surrounded by a wall, and with a *plaza* in the middle—every town of whatever size has its *plaza.* Here there was a church, with a thatched roof, differing only from the other houses by being a little larger, and having in front of it two upright posts, on which were hung a couple of cracked bells. This was the only public building of any pretensions. I am sorry to say that the priest seemed to spend most of his time in the *fonda,* and if all we heard was true, could not have been a very desirable pastor to his flock. But the clergy in this country are on the whole such a worthless body, that the superstition of the inhabitants must be very great to leave them any influence at all. Jim and this priest made friends, and they had a bottle of *caña* together, on the morning after our arrival, while Eckford and I went out for a walk.

But on trying to go out of the village, we were astonished to find that there seemed to be no outlet but the road by which we had entered, and which was so narrow that it could be barricaded by a cart, as was done at night. After some search we were directed to a hole in the wall, only big enough to let us creep through, which nevertheless every one had to make use of in leaving the town by that side. This was a precaution against a sudden attack by the Indians, of which that neighbourhood stands in constant dread.

But when once we had got out into the open, we were amply repaid for our trouble. The place stands at the base of the sierra which bounds the country to the west; and after our monotonous experience of flat plains covered by scorched grass, we were inexpressibly delighted to see again hills, and trees, and rocks, and to tread once more upon pebbles, and have the delightful sensation of climbing. As we ascended one of the lower hills, we agreed that the scenery was not unlike the Highlands of Scotland. There was actually a *burn*, a gurgling, rippling stream of crystal water, slipping through narrow gorges and sliding over granite shelves into deep foamy pools. There were flowers, too, among the rocks, scarlet verbenas, and others which seemed familiar, though I did not know their names, and patches of soft green turf, and large trees, their roots overgrown with brilliant cushions of moss, and their branches loaded with bright red fruits that reminded us of holly berries, and ferns, the first I had seen since leaving England. It was most refreshing; but when we turned round we saw nothing but the wide dead level of grass across which we were presently to steer our way, and I caught myself wishing that my friends had pitched their camp in this picturesque spot, which reminded us so of home.

So far as our business went, however, we might as well have never come here, for on inquiry we could hear no news of our horses. We applied for the aid of the judge of the peace, the chief legal dignitary of the place, who in private life exercised the functions of a general store-keeper. This gentleman seemed to enter with great zeal into our case, but only, as we soon found, for the purpose of informing us that he himself had some horses to sell. The look of these animals, and the price he demanded, deprived us of the hope of any further assistance in this quarter; and we set out for home, intending to make two days' good riding of it,—the distance being somewhat over a hundred miles,—so as to be back in time for Christmas. Jim said he couldn't live over another year in this country without a Christmas dinner.

Of course you will not suppose that it was anything like the Christmas weather at home. While you were sliding and snowballing, we were riding along in our flannel shirt sleeves, and great straw hats, inside of which we placed our handkerchiefs to keep off the rays of the sun blazing overhead in the cloudless sky. The country through which we were passing was flat as a pancake, and most wearily monotonous. For miles and miles you would see nothing but dry grass, in some places as high as your waist, in others short and black, after a recent fire. Not a tree in the horizon; only at intervals were little clumps of stunted bushes, and now and then our road took us past a *laguna*, or shallow lake, of muddy, brackish water, bordered with sickly-looking reeds. The smallest rock would have looked beautiful to us, but there was not even a pebble; the hard ground, however, was here and there dotted with bones, which are the stones of the Pampas.

This desert of grass, where a district might be said to be thickly populated if there were houses within ten miles of each other, was even more of a solitude than usual; for there was a rumour that the Indians were out again, and those who had anything to lose had fled with it to the shelter of the nearest town. We passed two abandoned *ranchos* in one day, and another which had been recently burned. So we were uncommonly hard up for Christmas fare, as we had taken nothing with us but biscuit, expecting as usual to be supplied on the way, and not a bit of meat could we now get for love or money, to Jim's exceeding disgust. The first day of our homeward journey he brought down with his revolver a young donkey, one of a herd which we met running wild, and was greatly comforted in spirit thereby. Certainly its flesh was a treat to us all. 'It went well,' as Jim said, with a chuckle and an oily smile that seldom appeared on his countenance, except when excited by the present or prospective savour of something to eat, for in other circumstances he seemed to have contracted something of *gaucho* stolidity. But our horses were already too much loaded with some purchases we had made at Riados, and we could not carry along enough of the donkey to suffice his voracious appetite all the way home. So next morning we thought ourselves very lucky to catch an armadillo, which we roasted in its shell for breakfast, and divided fairly, Jim having the shell to scrape, over and above his share. But this did not appease him, and he sighed to arrive at the station, where Desmond and the Simpsons had agreed to kill a cow between them, in order that Christmas might be kept in due style.

In the forenoon we caught sight of a native hut, a mile or so out of our line of march; and as the smoke rising from the roof seemed to promise that the owner was at home, we thought it worth while to turn aside to pay him a visit.

We found Mr. Gaucho standing in front of his door, doing nothing,—an accomplishment which the whole race are perfect masters of; and after the usual salutation, '*Ave Maria!*' and waiting to be asked to dismount, as the etiquette of the country is, we let our horses graze for a little, while we entered the hut, a low erection of wattled reeds, strengthened at intervals by rough posts, and thatched with *paja*, a kind of coarse grass. In the middle was a fire of logs, perhaps a couple of yards long, which are shoved forward as they burn away, so that they may go on burning for days. Round the fire were low, roughly cut benches, on which we seated ourselves at the courteous invitation of Mrs. Gaucho, a dark-hued young woman, who was herself sitting on a cow's skull, a cigarette in her mouth and a baby on her knee, the latter very like home babies, only of course darker, and with the *bombilla* of a *maté*-pot between its gums, instead of a coral. A pretty little girl, three or four years older, stood shyly in the corner, and looked wonderingly out of her great black eyes at the strangers.

Could they let us have any meat? No, nothing of the kind to be had, only some *masa mora*, or maize porridge. Was there any village near, where we could get some? ' *Quien sabe?* ' said the *gaucho*, with a shrug of his shoulders. But the hospitable couple would do what they could for us, and the goodwife, laying the baby in a wooden box hung from the roof by a cord, set about preparing the eternal *maté*, which it must be a poor hut indeed that does not possess. While it was being got ready, we were informed of all the news of the neighbourhood—how many lambs had died of the cold that season; how our host's master had left his *estancia*, and driven away his flocks, for fear of the Indians; how a jaguar—or tiger, as these animals are called out there—with two cubs had been seen not far off, and so forth.

Most of this, of course, I could not understand; but I tried to exercise my small stock of Spanish upon the little girl in the corner, asking her if she would come home to England with me and be my wife,—a proposal which she promptly and forcibly declined, and clung to her father, as if claiming his protection against such a monster as me. Jim was more successful in entering into the good graces of the master of the house, who, after a little talk, produced a bottle of *caña*, which Jim took to so willingly that Eckford made haste to put an end to the visit.

We said *Adios* to our entertainers, and went on our way, making towards a little patch of trees which Jim told us we must steer for, to recover our path. He professed to know every inch of the road; and as he had spent the last ten years of his life in the neighbourhood, we trusted him implicitly, though it was unfortunately evident that the *caña* had got a little into his head, causing him to be very dogmatic, and even more eloquent than usual upon the good things of home.

On we rode, nothing doubting but that the same night would bring us in sight of the station. About three o'clock we saw the line of trees which marked the course of a river we had to cross, on the last stage of our road; and passing through a marshy jungle, where the rank grass reached to our horses' heads, we came down upon the bank.

The river struck us as wider than it had seemed on our outward journey; and riding along, we looked in vain for the ford by which we had crossed it before, and which Jim assured us was not more than a mile or so down the stream. But when we had ridden more than three or four miles, our too confident guide bethought himself of looking at the sun, and suddenly pulling up, exclaimed—

'Here's a nice mess you've made of it!'

'What's the matter?' we cried, without wasting time in questioning the view he took of any mistake that might have been made.

'Matter!' said Jim; 'why, we're a matter of twenty miles out of the road, and I'll eat my horse if we get home by dinner-time on Christmas day.'

Jim's head was quite clear by this time; his disgust at this discovery had driven out of it the last fumes of the *caña*, and he plainly explained the mistake that had been made, in a grumbling tone which still seemed to lay the blame on us. Now that the sun was declining in the heavens, we saw that we had actually been riding south-west instead of north-east—in fact, almost in the same direction from which we had come in the morning. The appearance of the river was explained by its taking a bend higher up; and if we turned and made for the ford, we should find that we had added about forty miles to our journey.

Of course we were all very much annoyed. If I, to whom the journey was like a great picnic, was tired of it, what must have been the feelings of my companions, who were going through with it as a troublesome matter of business!

But Eckford did not waste any time in reproaching Jim, who, as has been seen, had taken care to be beforehand in throwing the blame off his own shoulders, and now thought it as well to say nothing further on the subject. The question was what to do; and here a map which Eckford carried, and the knowledge of the country which Jim professed, —not, as a rule, without reason,—agreed to show that our best course was to cross the river at this point, and then take a straight line for home. So this was settled, and I had an opportunity of seeing the way in which the want of a bridge may be supplied.

We dismounted and unsaddled, and Eckford's large mackintosh being spread out, the corners were tied up with thongs. Next, picking up three stout branches, which had probably been used for this purpose before, Jim tied them together in a triangular form with his lasso, and on this rude raft made fast the mackintosh. So the *pilota* was built; then we applied ourselves to load her, and a heavy cargo it was. Saddles, baggage, and clothes—for we now stripped; even our watches and revolvers. All that I had in the New World, except a change of clothes or so at the *estancia*, was on board this frail transport; so it may be imagined that I looked forward to the result of the voyage with no small anxiety. Bob Eckford took another means of conveying his purse and other valuables; he put them in his boots and hung them round the horse's neck. This seemed to me even more hazardous than the way in which I had ventured my property.

The *pilota* was launched, and Jim, holding in his hand the lasso attached to it, mounted bare-backed, in more senses than one, and rode into the water *à la* Lady Godiva. Away went the horse, puffing like a steam-tug, with the precious freight in tow. The river was deep and rapid, but a very short time decided the fate of the voyage. We had soon the extreme satisfaction of seeing our goods drawn up on *terra firma*, and the horse shaking himself like a dog on the other bank. Having tied it to a tree, Jim plunged into the river again, and came swimming across, hand over hand, in Indian fashion, or like a dog, to guide me, as a novice in this sort of work, with his counsel and assistance.

Ugh! It was cold, in spite of the great heat of the sun. I had been instructed to walk out as long as I could feel bottom. 'Now!' cries Jim; and obedient to his teaching, I catch hold of the horse's mane with one hand, and strike out with the other, my preceptor keeping close at hand. The horse is a ticklish one to manage in such circumstances, unaccustomed to this sort of work as he is. When he has lost his footing, instead of making straight for the opposite side, he tries to turn round, and begins to go down with the stream. 'Hold him fast!' yells Jim, quite unnecessarily, for I had no intention of letting him go. But in spite of our shouts, the animal still struggles to wheel round, and the situation becomes critical. You must on no account touch the bridle, they say, or the horse may become restive; and if once he gets his ears under the water, it is all up with him. But Jim comes to the rescue; he dashes a little water on the horse's head at the side to which he tries to turn, and the animal takes the hint, and, to my great relief, sets his face towards the bank, and goes forward in a business-like manner. I land in triumph, and am welcomed by Bob Eckford, who, not being a good swimmer, has crossed holding on to his horse's tail, and, without waiting to put on his clothes, is now sitting high and dry on the bank, smoking a cigar, and looking like a primeval philosopher.

But now came a sensational incident. As I was scrambling up the steep, muddy bank, Bob suddenly made my heart leap into my mouth by shouting out, 'A lion! a lion!' and rushed off towards the *pilota* where our arms were. To be attacked by a lion in such an extremely defenceless state, sounds like no joke; but to begin with, the name of lion is in this country given to the puma, and on the present occasion at least, this spurious pretender to the kingdom of the beasts showed himself an utter craven, flying at the very sight of us, so that the first and last glimpse I got of him was, a tawny-coloured beast, about the size of a big Newfoundland dog, disappearing into the bushes. Jim professed to be very ill satisfied that it had not stood an encounter with us, for he thought a lion steak would be very acceptable for supper, and the flesh of the puma is in fact not bad eating, resembling veal. He tried to make up for this disappointment by prowling about to have a shot at the variously tinted paroquets, which abounded on the banks, but was not able to hit one. None of my readers need be shocked at the notion. Parrot-pie was a favourite dish not only with Jim, but with other inhabitants of the camp, and you would not hesitate to shoot them if you were a farmer out there, and knew how much mischief can be done by these beautiful but unprincipled birds, coming in flocks as they do, and inviting themselves to dine rather too often on your maize.

When we had dressed, we sat still for a little and enjoyed this little bit of wood scenery. The banks, covered with a carpet of bright green grass; the trees, casting their chequered shade upon the masses of trailing shrubs beneath, made a picture which, in spite of high cactuses and other unfamiliar plants, and the gay and graceful little humming-birds flitting about among them, reminded us again of home, at least by its delightful contrast to the monotonous stretches of the camp. The smallest plantation here is indeed a treasure; and if I rejoiced to have my thoughts called back to dear old Sherwood forest, what must be the effect on settlers who are doomed to a long exile from the friendly scenes of their youth!

We would willingly have spent the night there; but as we had still an hour or two of daylight left, it was thought best to push a few miles farther on into the camp. So, after resting about an hour, we resumed our journey. But when at sunset we halted for the night, we began to regret having left the friendly shelter of the trees, for threatenings of a storm were only too plain. The day had been extremely hot, and a scorching north wind, like a blast from a furnace, had made us long for the cool of evening, as we jogged over these shadeless plains. Now came the ugly signs of a change. The air was stiflingly close, and thick with insects. To the south, the sky wore a strange dirty look, and gradually great masses of dense black cloud rose up and spread over it till it was covered as with a pall, except where a dark crimson glow marked the quarter in which the sun had just set. This broke up into lurid streaks, and when the last of these had died away the darkness quickly deepened, till it became so intense that we could not see our own fingers held up before our faces. The wind had fallen; there was an ominous silence, or rather a mysterious sound that might be called more still than silence, as if the spirits of the air were whispering under their breath some dreadful secret. Nothing else could we hear but the alarmed foxes and *biscachos* hurrying through the grass to their holes—they well knew what was in the wind.

Then came low rumbling sounds in the distance, as of an army marching to the battle-field, and we felt a soft, whispering rain falling about us. Suddenly a crash and a flash, like a signal-gun, gave

SPENDING THE NIGHT.—*The Pampas*, p. 112.

notice that the combat was opened, and the wind began to blow from the south-west with momentarily increasing vehemence. The rain grew heavier and heavier, the lightning glared all round us, and the thunder burst above our heads in sharp short claps, after each of which there was a momentary interval of awful silence. Soon the sky was all ablaze, and the merciless storm was discharging its full artillery of wind, rain, and hail upon us, as we stood shelterless on the open plain, and tried to keep our horses still; they did not appear terrified, but they turned round and fidgeted as if they wanted to run before the storm. We had made an attempt to light a fire under a sheepskin, but the flickering flames were blown out at the first breath of the Pampero. All we could do was to turn our backs to the blast, and wait till it passed over.

Unpleasant as our situation was, the sight was a magnificent one, and never to be forgotten. The air was full of electricity. Our horses' ears were tipped with a bright shimmering light, even the threads on the fringe of Jim's *poncho*, waving in the wind, shone and danced about like fire-flies. This we saw in the occasional glimpses of darkness, but for the most part we were almost blinded by the lightning, which came from every point of the compass, now in vivid flashes that lit up the camp for miles around, now in a dazzling stream that seemed to run along half the horizon, and now in balls of fire that burst like a rocket, scattering rays in all directions. Add the mingled roar of wind and thunder, and the torrents of drenching rain, and you will have some idea of the horror of the scene, and the wretched plight of us poor benighted travellers exposed to all this rage of the elements.

About midnight the storm began to abate. The wind sank, the rain ceased, the pale watery moon came out, the *lagunas* resounded with the croaking of innumerable frogs, and the whole plain seemed alive with the cries of animals set free to wander in search of their food. We huddled together in our soaking clothes, and tried to sleep as best we could, and to dream that it was really Christmas Eve.

CHAPTER VII.

OUR CHRISTMAS DINNER.

STIFF, cold, and uncomfortable, I awoke next morning about five o'clock, and saw the streaks of light brightening in the east. Then the Christmas sun appeared, raising his round red face through the grass, and showing how it bent and rippled beneath the gentlest of breezes. I rose, and strolled a short way to stretch myself, and enjoy the fresh cool air, as well as to look at the traces of the storm, and to think a little, for there is a good deal to think about on one's first Christmas spent so far away from home. When I came back, I found Bob Eckford sitting half-dressed, smoking a pipe, while his shirt and coat were hung out to dry on the back of a horse.

'A merry Christmas!' said I, in the cheerful tone which is affected on such occasions.

'A merry Christmas, indeed!' replied he. 'I call it a miserable Christmas.'

All we could do was to make the best of it. There was no fear that our clothes would not dry soon enough; and as for keeping Christmas in proper style, why, with the thermometer at ninety-five in the shade, that might be done any day just as well as another; at least with this reflection we tried to comfort ourselves.

While Bob and I were looking to the horses, we noticed that Jim had disappeared. Presently he came back from the direction of the *laguna*, and we at once were struck by some odd change that seemed to have come over him. We soon saw what it was; *he had been washing his face and hands*. He looked quite ashamed of himself, too, as he came up and received our congratulations.

'Well, what are you laughing at?' he said. 'Christmas comes but once a year.'

'Bravo, Jim!' cried Bob. 'Why, man, it's a pity there isn't a Lord Mayor in these parts, for he would be bound to ask you to dinner when you come out so swell.'

'It's a pity there isn't a decent Christian dinner in these parts,' growled Jim, who evidently took it very much to heart that we were so far off from the fatted calf which was no doubt being killed for us at home. 'You might as well do away with Christmas altogether, if it means nothing but hard biscuit and dish-water.'

'Cheer up, Jim; "there's pippins and cheese to come?"'

'Where?' said Jim so earnestly, that we both burst out laughing. Jim wasn't up in Shakespeare.

But certainly it seemed a bad business that nothing more could be done in the way of keeping Christmas properly, and as we rode along it was proposed that we should make an effort to get a bit of beef somehow or other. To this we all agreed; Jim, because the want of beef seemed really to prey upon his mind; I, because it was the first Christmas I had ever spent away from home; and Bob, because he was the most good-natured fellow in the world, and was always willing to agree to everything. But it was mighty fine talking; the cats might as well agree that the mice were to come to them and be eaten. Not a sign of a horned beast was to be seen, and in desperation Jim began to cast eyes of longing upon my horse, which was a stumbling old brute, fit for little else than the shambles. Jim's favourite form of asseveration was to say, 'I'll eat my boots!' and he never came nearer meaning it than that day, when he offered to eat any amount of boots if ever again we caught him in the open camp on Christmas day. It was a lesson to us all not to travel on the Pampas without at least a supply of *charqui* or dried meat, to fall back upon in case of need.

In the afternoon we came in sight of a few huts, and rode up to them, hoping to find beef. But no beef was to be found. The inhabitants had mostly disappeared, but in the only decent house of the place we found a band of *gauchos*, armed profusely with knives, lassos, *bolcadores*, and moustaches, who, under the pretence of looking out for the Indians, were smoking cigarettes and drinking *maté*. We accepted their invitation to join them in this dissipation, and in a dish of *masa mora*, but Jim declared that such poor stuff only made him think of beef more anxiously. All the same, however, he contrived to do with a good deal of what was going.

Eckford fancied one of the *gauchos'* horses, and not willing to return home empty-handed, wished to buy it, but the man would not even hear of parting with it. Indeed, a *gaucho* without his horse would be as much at sea as a sailor is on land; no Londoner out of the reach of omnibuses could be more helpless, no hunter in the middle of Fleet Street more disconsolate. Utterly idle and useless on foot, these fellows will do anything and go anywhere when mounted. I never saw one sleeping on horseback, but this probably is because they are never thoroughly awake anywhere else. They certainly use their saddles as beds, and so may be said to spend most of their life on them. A native's saddle or *recado* is the whole, or the greater part, of his furniture. It is a cumbrous-looking affair, composed of several layers of cloth and hide, with a wooden seat over all, which takes a long time to put on, and gives a great deal of trouble by constantly requiring to be adjusted; but then it must be remembered that expedition is an idea totally outside of a *gaucho's* comprehension. If any stirrups are used, they are heavy triangular ones, less for use than ornament. It is more common to have merely a thong with a knot at the end which the rider inserts between his first and second toes. Boots are not *de rigeur* in a native's dress, and when he wears them there is an opening at the toes, which your true *gaucho* makes great use of in dealing with horses, and by constant practice is often more expert with these members than some Englishmen are with their fingers.

A word more about horses while I am on the subject. The camel has been called the ship of the desert, but in this country it is hard to say what useful function the horse is not called on to fulfil at times. I have seen a man fishing in the sea on horseback, and a milkman in Buenos Ayres kneeling on his horse in the middle of the pails, as he went round and delivered his wares. A common way of thrashing among the natives is to strew the corn over an enclosure, into which they turn a herd of wild mares; and in the same way horses are used to trample down wet earth for making it into bricks. I have been told, though I do not vouch for this, that when a *gaucho* wishes to churn butter, he merely ties a bladder full of the raw material to his horse's tail, and sets off at full gallop; and that he cooks a beef-steak also, by putting it under his saddle for an hour or two. And when a horse's days of general usefulness are over, he may be killed and eaten with great relish by his sorrowing master. Stay! this must be a calumny. I doubt if a native would partake of his own horse. There is often a great deal of mutual affection between the four-legged and the two-legged animal.

Though our horses were tired, we were anxious to push on as near home as possible that day; so, after a couple of hours' halt, we left the village, and struck out once more into the pathless sea of green. By this time we had given up hopes of our beef, and were looking forward to another meagre banquet, which so weighed on Jim's spirits, that he rode along silent and downcast, and when Bob asked him what he was thinking of, answered, 'Pork sausages!' in a tone of profound melancholy that would have melted the heart of an Old Bailey barrister. But one minute afterwards his eye was lit up by a gleam of hope; he rose in his stirrups, shaded his brow with his hand, then frantically stretched it out, exclaiming in a loud whisper,—

'An animal! an animal!'

'An animal indeed, or I'll eat Jim's boots!' said Bob, and sure enough there was a four-legged, two-horned creature lying calmly within three hundred yards of us, between a *laguna* and a little clump of bushes, chewing the cud of reflection in a manner which showed it all too unconscious of our blood-thirsty desires. As we cautiously approached, it rose to welcome us, swishing its tail a little, as if giving a final touch to its toilet. Then it was a civilised bit of beef, therefore some one's property, and not available for our needs! But when we got close enough to see that it was an almost full-grown heifer, Jim triumphantly declared that it was not branded, and so might fall a lawful prey.

Here was beef, indeed, for the catching; but we—two of us at least—were not quite sure about the catching of it. Bob and I could not realize the phenomenon of a cow without an owner, and had our home notions of the rights of property strong upon us. Jim laughed our scruples to scorn, and declared that it was no doubt a calf that had strayed from the Indians, and set up on the Pampas on its own account. On the other hand, we urged that young beasts were not always branded, and suggested an owner taking a *siesta* in the grass near at hand, or posting after us from the village we had just left. Jim swept such arguments to the winds by offering to eat the animal, horns and all, if it belonged to anybody rather than to us. The prospect of beef was indeed sweet, and Bob began to give in; then I did not care to oppose my companions. And it was necessary to make an immediate decision, for the *vaquillona*, after apparently satisfying herself that we were not worthy of her acquaintance, was leisurely making off. The jury at once brought their deliberations to a close, and passed sentence of death upon her; but that we were not quite sure in our minds of the lawfulness of our proceedings, was plain from the careful way in which we looked round to see that no one was in sight, before proceeding to execution. As for me, I wasn't at all comfortable about it, and felt quite like being at school again, and expecting a master to come round the corner and catch me smoking.

Our victim was soon roused from its dream of

security. Galloping on each side, Bob Eckford and Jim lassoed it by the horns, and brought it to the ground, and I was called on to do the rest. That was a part of the business I never could get used to. To see the poor beast struggling helplessly, and look into its mild eyes as it gave a last kick and a faint bellow of despair, was always too much for me, and I turned away my head when I plunged the knife in its throat, and made such a bungle of the business, that Jim was moved to use strong language, and declared that I deserved never to taste meat again till the day of my death. He sprang off his horse, and finished the job in a workmanlike manner. Then, before the breath was out of the beast's body, he cut off the *matambre*, as they call the piece off the ribs which is most easily come by, also a juicy steak or two for his own private eating. These he strung upon the spit which travellers on the Pampas always carry about with them by way of complete kitchen range; and, leaving the rest of the carcase for whoever would, we resumed our journey, rejoiced to have provided ourselves with materials for a Christmas dinner, and still more rejoiced that we had done so without any one seeing us. For the fact was, that we had been engaged in something very like robbery.

'But it's better to be hung than starved,' said

Jim, regarding the beef with eyes that had a touch of sentiment in them; 'and it's more heathenish to go without beef on Christmas than to help yourself when a beast is so silly as to get in your way.'

By such arguments Jim silenced all scruples, and who can say that most conquerors and slaughterers on a large scale have had more reason to back them up?

It never rains but it pours, they say, and certainly we were in luck that afternoon, for when we had ridden a little farther, we found in the grass a nest of ostrich eggs, twenty or thirty of them lying in a circle, and Mrs. Ostrich away from home, marketing or gossiping with some of her neighbours. So we helped ourselves to as many as we could stow away among our baggage, or in the breasts of our shirts; nothing could be more useful to us. You had only to bore a little hole in the top of these eggs, put in a bit of lard, and boil them on the ashes without further ceremony. Jim's spirits rose greatly. He began to entertain vivid hopes of a pudding, for he had found some stray melons growing wild at one of the deserted *ranchos* we passed, which he proposed to cut up into small pieces, to serve instead of plums. Only two indispensable things were wanting—a cloth, and a pot to boil the pudding in. As to the former, Jim volunteered to lend his shirt,—an offer which we promptly and firmly rejected. The second difficulty seemed harder to get over, and our swivel-eyed friend ruminated upon it in vain.

Towards sunset we came to a deserted station where we resolved to camp. There was a *corral* fenced with rough posts, a broken hut surrounded by a trench, and, what was of far more consequence than any other accommodation, a well of good water. We turned our horses into the *corral*, and hastened to scrape together materials for a fire. I fear I may shock some polite readers by telling them what is the fuel to which one is generally reduced on the Pampas. It is nothing more or less than dry cow-dung, which makes a better fire than you would suppose, and is most valuable in a country where sticks are not to be picked up every day. From the accounts of eastern travellers, I understand that this use of it is not confined to South America.

So we lit our fire, began to cook our meal, and prepared to spend the evening jovially. But my uneasiness about the beef of which we had possessed ourselves had not lessened during the journey; and when I got Bob Eckford alone for a minute or two, I soon won him over to my view of the matter. We could be by no means sure that this cow had not an owner. If the owner found out his loss and followed us, the consequences might be unpleasant; even Jim admitted that. In the village we had given out where we were going, and had been heard making earnest inquiries for beef. Apart from the usual inconveniences of being chased as cattle-stealers, we had a considerable sum of money with us, which, after what we had seen of the native authorities, we had no desire to let them get hold of. These were the arguments I used, but I confess that my strongest feeling in the matter was a scruple about what at home would be looked upon as a disreputable crime. I had not been out long enough to grow accustomed to the free and easy ways of camp life; and I so far succeeded in gaining over my companions, that they saw we had not done wisely in leaving that carcase near our track to bear witness against us. So it was agreed that two of us should go back and drag the body into the *laguna*, or hide it among the bushes, while one stayed and prepared the Christmas banquet on which we had set our hearts.

We drew lots with blades of grass, and Bob Eckford had the longest, so he was told off to mind the cooking, and Jim and I lost no time in retracing our way to the spot where we had left the dead cow.

By this time the brief twilight was over, and the

moon was shining brightly upon the grassy waves of the Pampas. As we rode silently along, and heard the owls hooting and the foxes barking on each side of us, I found my thoughts running away to Christmas at home—to the ivied church, and the carols in the frosty darkness, and the dear old lanes covered with crackling snow, and the cheery faces round the festive fire. In their merriment, did those I had left behind ever spare a minute to wonder what I was doing? At this moment the cloth would perhaps have been taken away, and my father was rising to drink to absent friends. Oh, nonsense! It would now be quite another time of day in England, and as likely as not, wet, foggy weather, while half my friends would probably be laid up with indigestion or influenza. With such prosaic business on hand, I must not allow myself to be so sentimental; and soon, indeed, I was brought out of my reveries by my horse stumbling over a little heap of bones, and nearly throwing me over his head.

'Now then!' said Jim, as if I had injured him; 'people as keeps their eyes inside their head must expect to have a crack on the outside of it.'

'You were thinking about something too, Jim,' said I, trying to pass the matter off pleasantly, and wondering whether my companion and I had no ideas which we might profitably and pleasantly exchange at such a time. Perhaps he had some one at home who was the lodestar of all his dreams.

'Thinking! yes,' growled Jim. 'I was thinking I would like to give all I am ever likely to get out of this blessed country, for a cut of a good fat ham and a mouthful of porter.'

Clearly Jim's soul was not poetical, and in my present mood I was not inclined to talk of hams; so we rode on in silence till we came to the *laguna*, on the other side of which lay the object of our quest, and beyond we could see twinkling a light or two in the village. Here a flock of plovers rose at our approach, and hovered round us, uttering their mournful cry, *teeru, tairo, teeru, tairo*, which, however striking from a poetical point of view, was not at all in harmony with our desire to call no attention to our business. It seemed as if the troublesome creatures would not leave us; but before Jim had time to tell them fully and forcibly his opinion of their proceedings, a new danger excited our apprehensions. A small band of horsemen were galloping towards us, attracted by the cry of the birds. We were in full view in the moonlight, and for a minute we stood still, not knowing whether they were friends or foes, and I heard the click of Jim's revolver.

' But when the new-comers drew near, we recognised them as a band of *gauchos*,—in fact, the same men that we had fallen in with earlier in the day.

'*Quien vive?*' they called out, halting at a few paces distant from us, and Jim put back his revolver into his belt, and gave a grunt. He had a supreme contempt for the *gauchos*.

My companion now came to the front and carried on a colloquy with the new-comers, from time to time letting me know what they were talking about.

The men began by telling us that they had come out to look for the Indians, who were close at hand. Why were we so rash as to be wandering about? Jim replied that we were looking out for one of our men who was coming after us, and whom we expected to join us somewhere hereabouts. To this they said that he would be sure to hear of the Indians, and make for the nearest settlement. No, Jim thought; he was a bold fellow, and not all the Indians in the country would keep him from coming on. The *gauchos* argued quite violently on this point. They were certain the man would not come; the Indians were close at hand; we were not safe in going about alone; they insisted on accompanying us to our camp, and spending the night with us. They said they wished to protect us. I believe the real truth was, they wanted us to protect them. In fact, they were so pressing in their kindness, that to avoid arousing suspicion, we were obliged to turn and go with them.

I could not understand why Jim, who had laughed at our fears of the cow getting us into a scrape, now showed himself so reluctant to give up the search for it. But he explained to me, as we went along, a reason for keeping these fellows out of our camp, which had not struck me in my innocence and inexperience. The *gauchos* were sharp enough in all matters relating to making free with other people's property; and if they saw us cooking beef *with the hide on*, they would guess it was not our own animal which we were disposing of in such a wasteful and luxurious fashion. Perhaps it was their cow we had been helping ourselves to, and in that case they would be sure to know the taste of it. So Jim's conscience was at length awakened, and he racked his brains for some way of getting rid of our unwelcome guests. But they were not to be got rid of. They assured us they didn't mind taking any amount of trouble to look after our safety.

We arrived in sight of the deserted station, and saw Bob Eckford's form bending over a great fire which he had managed to heap up. No doubt he was roasting the beef, our Christmas beef, which we wished now we had never set eyes on. But

Jim's ingenuity, after all, stood us in good stead. He informed the *gauchos* that our friend was a terribly fierce fellow—good-natured Bob!—and that he was sure to shoot at any strangers who might approach him in the darkness. This had a great effect on our companions, and they agreed to pull up and wait, while Jim rode on and announced us.

So we stood for a few minutes at a respectful distance from the hut, and smoked our cigarettes in patience. Presently we heard a whistle, and Jim's voice shouting '*Esta bueno!*' We rode forward, and when we got within the glow of the campfire there was not a sign of beef to be seen.

Our friends seemed to be very much disappointed when they found we had nothing to offer them but hard biscuits, ostrich eggs, and the everlasting *maté*. However, they made the best of it, and sat round our fire, smoking cigarettes and telling us stories of their daring adventures with the Indians—*stories!* We began to wonder if they were ever going to sleep; but at last they curled themselves up in their *ponchos*, and lay down to rest on their saddles, we volunteering to keep watch for the first part of the night.

As soon as they were all asleep, Bob and I stole down into the ditch, where we found Jim already hard at work, devouring the cold beef. We whipped out our knives and joined him, and when we had finished we buried the fragments out of sight. In this uncomfortable way we ate our Christmas dinner on the Pampas.

Next morning the *gauchos* left us, and we decided to push on for home. When we got there we found all well, and heard something which interested us. Some time before, Desmond had bought a few head of cattle from a neighbour of ours,—that is to say, a settler who lived about thirty miles off,—but had not had an opportunity of fetching them home. In consequence of a message from him to say that the Indians had been looking about his place, and that he would not answer for the safety of our animals, one of the *peons* had been sent to drive them over in our absence. On the way, he had been frightened out of his life by what he took for a troop of Indians in the distance, and had run away from his charge with great zeal, but returned on finding that the alarm had been caused by nothing more dangerous than half-a-dozen wild horses. He recovered all the cows but one heifer, which had strayed somewhere in the neighbourhood where we were travelling on Christmas afternoon.

So that, after all, it was probably our own beef we had stolen to make a Christmas dinner, and thus a weight was removed from our consciences, at the same time that a capital joke was established against us; and in camp-life, a joke, like many other things, is a great piece of good fortune, and gets made the best of.

This was the first and the last time that I ever stole a cow.

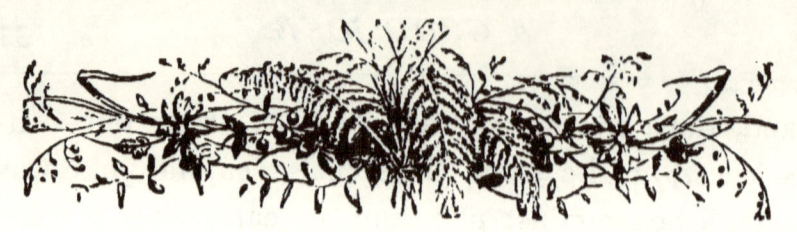

CHAPTER VIII.

A PARTY IN CAMP.

LIFE at a solitary station in camp is apt to seem a little monotonous at times, especially when, as was the case with my hosts, the settlers are obliged to restrict their operations for fear of Indians, and for the same reason find it necessary to keep at home as much as they can. The best of friends will grow a little tired of each other when thrown so very much together as we were; and no doubt the greatest hardship men in Desmond's and Eckford's position had to put up with was want of society, which caused every casual visitor to be hailed like a bosom friend. So we were all glad of an invitation to a party at our neighbours', the Simpsons, which party I will give some account of, as anything of this sort was in itself an unusual event in our existence, and there was a special cause which makes it very unlikely that any of us will forget that evening.

The form in which this invitation was conveyed is perhaps one not usual in the higher society of Europe, so I will give it as a specimen of the manners and customs of our community. The younger Simpson rode over one afternoon, and not finding any of us at home except Senecio, who 'answered the door,' or rather who didn't answer the door, first, because he was asleep, and second, because for the nonce there was no door to answer—it had been taken down to be mended; after waiting, then, an hour or so, and making himself a *maté* and some cigarettes, the visitor went away, leaving upon the table, as a card, a pair of boots which he had borrowed from Desmond, and the following note written on the inside of a newspaper wrapper, the only available scrap of paper he could find lying about :—

'Messrs. Simpson present their compliments, and beg to state that they propose next Wednesday evening to hold a high-class symposium, at which the presence of your ugly mugs will not be objected to.

'*P.S.*—Can you lend us your big pot?'

To this we duly replied that, after consulting our list of engagements, we found that we were all free for that evening, and would be happy to give them the pleasure and honour of our company and the big pot's; to which Bob Eckford added that he hoped they would have a good dinner, as he meant to eat nothing for three days before, lest he should fail to do justice to their hospitality.

The party was originally fixed to take place on Christmas Eve, but it had been put off till the last night of the year on account of the shearing, which with the Simpsons, as well as with ourselves, was later than usual. But it was understood that, in defiance of the calendar, this festival was to be kept with all the honours peculiar to Christmas; plum-pudding, at all events, was distinctly promised by the givers of the feast.

So, in high spirits, we three, attended by Senecio, who was to wait at table, and to that intent had had his hair combed out and his gloves washed, set out about four o'clock for Belvoir Castle. Such was the pretentious name given to their place by the Simpsons, though you are not to imagine that their accommodation was much more stately than ours. It consisted of a square enclosure surrounded by a ditch, at one corner of which they had just built a circular fort of turf, about twelve feet in diameter, with loopholes on every side, with the view of entertaining the Indians successfully, if any should come that way. Besides, there were two sheds, and a sheep and a horse *corral*. On the roof of the fort was hoisted a Union Jack, with which our hosts always marked Sundays and holidays.

We were most hospitably welcomed by the Simpsons, fine young fellows of the true blue-eyed, fair-bearded Saxon type, and after refreshing ourselves with *maté*, were shown over the 'improvements,' and spent a good deal of time in criticizing them, especially the fort, discussing the probability of the Indians coming back, the sheep, the wool, and of course the weather. But the main point of interest was the banqueting-hall, a long rough shed that had been put up for the shearers, and now, all traces of business having been removed from it, was decorated for the occasion as well as the resources of the establishment would permit. The main feature of these decorations was supplied by blankets, which, being of a bright red colour, made a great show hung at intervals along the walls, though, when a slight wind arose a little later in the evening, they caused some inconvenience by flapping about in an undecided manner. The walls were further adorned by bunches of thistles, as the nearest substitute for holly, by a couple of deer's heads, and by all the guns and pistols of the establishment arranged in a striking device. Over the door was worked A MERRY CHRISTMAS, in large letters of prairie grass. But the chief ornament of the place was the jolly, friendly faces of our hosts, on which we could plainly read that their hearts were filled with a seasonable warmth of hospitality.

All the guests arrived in good time. Besides ourselves, there were three other bold Britons, also a German called Schmidt, a name which was not altogether unfamiliar to us, and a little American who was called Major, but I don't remember, if I ever heard, what his name was. According to his account of himself, which he was by no means backward in giving in full, he had been in almost every line in life without success, in his own country, and had come out here to try sheep-farming for a year or two. His last engagement had been in the Confederate army during the unhappy civil war then just ended; and he puzzled me very much by the dubious language in which he described the nature of his services.

'My conduct on the field of battle, sir,' he said, 'was *notorious*.'

'Indeed!' said I, and to myself: 'if I were you, I should say as little about it as possible.'

'Yes, sir,' he went on with great complacency, 'my conduct was so *notorious* that it was noticed in all the journals.'

To this I did not know what to say, but my new friend went on to enlighten me.

'In fact, sir, I got a medal for my *notorious* conduct on the field of battle.'

'Oh!' I exclaimed, for it suddenly struck me that the difficulty between us lay in the use of the word *notorious*. But the valiant Major seemed to think that my exclamation was a note of admiration for his prowess, and he took me forthwith into great familiarity and confidence, and before long had informed me that his mother was the author of the celebrated ode to Jefferson Davis, published in the *Minxville Independent*, and that the suit of clothes he had on cost him a hundred and fifty dollars in New York.

The German was a quiet elderly man, who did not appear to speak English very copiously; but he had an enormous pipe with him, constructed by himself out of a hollowed bit of wood and the *bombilla* of a *maté* apparatus, and was quite happy so long as he was allowed to puff away at it in peace. Of the Englishmen, one was a man well on in life, who had been in the country for thirty years, and, having married there, had become almost a native himself in dress and manner, though he was evidently not ill pleased to be among his own countrymen again. His name was Darrell. The other two, Clarke and

Hett, were young fellows more lately settled in the colony, but who had already acquired the frank and roughly friendly ways encouraged by camp-life, where grown-up men behave somewhat like hearty schoolboys, whose development in the direction of ceremoniousness has been checked at the age of seventeen, and whose boisterous good fellowship has been perhaps too little refined by the influence of female society. Clarke was the son of a man who had made money in the colony many years before, but having lost it all in England, had recently returned, bringing his family with him. It appeared plain that the young fellow was not long from home, for he was festively attired in a cricketing suit of white flannel. The rest of us were in full Pampas costume of worn tweeds, pea-jackets, Crimean shirts, and the like; two gentlemen had top-boots on, and might be considered the swells of the party.

At seven o'clock, punctually, that is, not more than half an hour on one or the other side of it, Senecio, his mouth on full grin, announced that dinner was ready, and brought forth to the well a tin basin and towels, in order that the assembled company, who had been sitting with their legs dangling in the ditch, might wash their hands and otherwise prepare themselves for the banquet. This did not occupy much time; then, our hosts leading the way, we took each other's arms, and proceeded, two and two, into the festal shed, which Eckford at once christened 'Noah's Ark.'

The decorations were pronounced eminently satisfactory, and the appearance of the table was all that could be expected in the circumstances. Of course the main difficulty in such an entertainment was a scarcity of plate, and it was one of the conditions of the invitation that every gentleman should contribute his share to that department. So, as the guests rode over that afternoon, you would have seen a knife and fork sticking out of each man's pocket, a plate or two disposed somewhere about him, and a mug hanging from his horse's head-stall; in fact, we somewhat resembled a band of great school children going out for a treat. The main part of the treat, however, in our case was not cake, but *bread*. Actually bread had been got from Villa Grande, and a great treat it was to us after our long experience of dry biscuit; ay, and there was butter too, and a large demijohn of peach jam, or *dulce*, as it was called. You may be sure we did not throw away many of these precious crumbs upon our dogs, several of whom had accompanied their masters on such a congenial expedition, and sat round the table a little distance off, respectfully awaiting their share in the entertainment. Beef they might have as much as they pleased; but not bread for them. Beef there was in plenty—*cela va sans dire*—and mutton cutlets with the tomato sauce which Pickwick has rendered famous, but which, to tell the truth, were probably better cooked by Mrs. Bardell than by our entertainers. Then came a pair of roast ducks, or rather one fowl and one duck, the hosts explaining that they had tried to shoot two, but in vain. Fish was somewhat sparely represented by a tin of sardines, and there was also some preserved soup, rather spoiled by over-boiling on the part of Master Senecio, but we were not disposed to be critical. Last of all there was the pudding, a true triumph of art over difficulties, baked, however, in a tin dish, for a clean and whole cloth to boil it in had proved an insurmountable difficulty. When I add that there was also the successful novelty of a melon pie, it will be seen that we could only have ourselves to blame if we did not make good cheer. Stop! I have forgotten to mention the vegetables, which consisted solely of *chocolos* or green corn cobs, boiled and served in a pitcher, which afterwards did duty as a hot water jug when the dessert was placed on the table.

Upon these viands we fell to with the hearty

appetite that camp-life gives, and which not even the continual round of *asado* and biscuit can blunt, though of course these unwonted luxuries gave it a fresh edge. So for an hour there was a great clatter of knives and spoons, as a running accompaniment to a perfect Babel of chattering and laughing.

I was a little unfortunate in the man who sat next to me, Mr. Darrell, to wit, whose long sojourn in the colony had not tended to make him a pleasant companion. Indians, locusts, droughts, fires, frosts, and hail-storms had taught him the fallaciousness of human hopes, and made him somewhat cynical and gloomy, when he abandoned his ordinary taciturnity; so, as I was a stranger, he felt bound to entertain me with an account of all the misfortunes and afflictions which I might expect to fall in with before leaving the country. It seemed that if I escaped being tortured by the Indians, or bitten by a serpent, I was sure to get in the way of a poisonous thorn which could only be recognised by its effects when the victim was past recovery; or, failing this, a fever would lay hold of me which I should never be able to shake off all my days. If I survived sufficiently to be able to start for home, I was to look out for one of the swampy spots by river banks, in which the horses of unaccustomed travellers were almost certain to sink up to the neck; but should I by any chance overcome all these dangers so far as to reach Buenos Ayres again, I might expect that a revolution would break out before I could take ship, and that I should be murdered by some zealous patriot, for the sake of my watch and purse. All this he told me with an air of kindly interest which was rather discouraging, and I wondered much how all these men looked so healthy and full of spirits, in a land where so many dangers beset even the temporary visitor. I was fain to comfort myself by thinking that there are croakers in all countries, and by observing that the troubles of life had not injured Mr. Darrell's appetite.

Dinner was got over with no other mishap than Senecio's upsetting a bowl of soup on the expectant nose of one of the dogs, and being so struck, first with alarm and then with admiration, when the plum-pudding was set on fire, that he forgot his duty of cleaning the plates without delay—for they had to be cleaned between each course—and drew down upon him the dreadful threat that he should not taste of the pudding if he did not mind what he was about. The dishes were at last cleared away; a jug of *caña*, with sugar, hot and cold water, and a jar of tobacco, were put on the table, and the company prepared to spend the evening.

This *caña* or sugar-cane rum is the chief alcoholic drink of the Pampas, and by itself is enough to have been the ruin of many a good man. Too many Englishmen are always tippling at it, and of course they are not slow to find an excuse for their glass upon all occasions. It is said to be good to open the eyes in the morning, and to shut them at night; to warm you in cold weather, and to cool you when it is hot; to give an appetite before meals, and to help digestion after them; to keep off infection, to cure sickness, and so forth. The fact is, that with the active out-of-door life in bracing air, and the plentiful food, a healthy man does not require stimulants in this country, while the loneliness and monotony often afford a too powerful temptation to excessive drinking. Desmond and Eckford had the sense to use no spirit in their house, unless for some special reason; but this rule was, unfortunately, not the universal one. I don't forget the way in which the American Major received my statement that I was an abstainer. 'Oh, you are, are you!' he said in a tone which was a mixture of unmistakeable pity and disdain; and I had clearly sunk so much in his good esteem that I had the weakness to feel ashamed of myself, and to go on to claim the merit of not having taken the pledge. But my cowardice was duly punished.

'Don't say another word, sir,' was his comment. 'I can understand a man that has taken the pledge because he thinks drinking isn't right; but a man that doesn't drink because he won't when he may, why—an Indian's an angel to him.'

This sentiment the speaker sent home by a good pull at his mug, and several of the others followed his example. But I hold to my opinion that this *caña* is sickening, maddening stuff, not worth drinking even in moderation. For the minority of two, who did not indulge in *caña*, there was *maté*, and I had the new experience of drinking, or rather *sucking*, the toasts of the evening through a *bombilla*.

These toasts were given with all due honours. First, 'The Queen and the Royal Family,' with a special bumper to the health of 'the young Wales' just born. Then, out of compliment to two of the party who were not Britons, the 'President of the United States,' 'and all the Kings and Queens of Germany.' Next, somebody proposed, ' The *present* Government of the Argentine Republic;' and this was drunk as a matter of form, but without much enthusiasm, which, however, burst forth in full warmth when *the* toast of the evening came on, ' Prosperity to the frontier settlements!' Then followed in quick succession, ' Our absent friends,' ' Our noble hosts,' ' Our noble guests,' ' Our faithful *peons*,' ' Our lambs,' ' Our horses,'

'Our noble selves,' who were all separately and emphatically declared to be 'jolly good fellows, which nobody can deny.'

This led the way to the musical portion of the evening, which, for lack of any ladies to join, directly succeeded the dessert, and was sustained with more zeal than harmony. Eckford's concertina was called into requisition, and we had several rattling songs of the Christy Minstrel type, those being most in favour which had the loudest and longest choruses, while at intervals Eckford and the German gave us a good old ballad or other melody of a more sentimental character. If any bewildered wanderer had chanced to come within half a mile of us while this concert was going on, he would probably have fled in terror before finding that he had to do with human beings, and neither fiends nor Indians. At one time, indeed, we ourselves were rather alarmed; for, as we ended a chorus, we heard a strange noise without, that seemed to echo back our merriment in unearthly tones. We rushed out, and found that Senecio, who was supposed to be washing up the dishes in an *al fresco* scullery, had taken to testifying his delighted interest in the proceedings by yelling and beating time on a pewter mug, while he capered about to the great danger of our miscellaneous crockery. He was forthwith dragged in, and forced on his bended knees to drink the glorious, pious, and immortal memory of Old King Cole in a glass of sugar-and-water, a ceremony which, as might be supposed, he performed with great gusto. By this time we were all rather hoarse, so we drew round the fire, and settled down to story-telling and asking riddles, in quite the orthodox Christmas party fashion. These latter, as usual, were more remarkable for ingenuity than for novelty; but one of them, propounded by the American Major, fixed itself in my mind. The question was—If every morning at ten o'clock a diligence leave Cordova for Rosario, and another leave Rosario for Cordova, each taking three days exactly to do the journey, how many diligences would a man who travelled one way meet coming from the opposite direction? I was not taken in, because I had been warned beforehand that our American friend made a point of proposing this puzzle to every stranger he fell in with, as soon as occasion offered, and the difficulty had been explained to me. But as nine out of ten of the people to whom I have since put the same question have given the same answer, and that a wrong one, I hereby present it to the ingenuity of my readers, assuring them that it is more difficult than it looks.

"'How many are there on the road already when you start!' chuckled the Major; and in this point, which almost every one is apt to overlook, lies the knot of the puzzle.

The longest story told was an account which Darrell gave us of some of his early experiences. I afterwards noted down what I could remember of it, and it is worth reporting, to show the difficulties which the first English settlers had often to encounter in the troubled state of politics which seems almost natural to this part of the world, where earthquakes and thunderstorms are scarcely more common or more destructive than wars and revolutions.

When Darrell first came to the River Plate, he had an *estancia* in the province of Entre Rios, and for ten years was moderately prosperous. But at the end of that time civil war broke out, and the district where he lived was ravaged by no less than three hostile armies. A battle seemed imminent not many miles from his house, but he did not intend to get out of the way, as most of his neighbours had done. Then a decree was issued by one of the hostile generals, that all the *estancias* round about should be abandoned by their owners within forty-eight hours. All the *peons* fled at once, but still Darrell remained, resolved to assert his rights to the last.

When the two days of grace had expired, a troop of men rode up to the *estancia*. After the usual '*Buenos dias*,' the officer inquired if the proclamation of his general had been received, and then asked how Darrell had dared to disobey it.

'Because, *señor*,' was the reply, 'as an Englishman I am under the protection of the British Government, and refuse to leave my property.'

At this the officer hesitated, and thought it as well to go back for further instructions, but soon returned with peremptory orders to use force if necessary. Darrell saw that further expostulation was useless,—resistance, of course, was out of the question; so, saddling his favourite horse, he rode away, leaving his house just as it was, with the doors open. Two days afterwards it was burned to the ground, and a fierce battle fought on the outskirts of his camp.

Darrell remained for some time in Gualeguaychu; but as the war still continued, and it was impossible for him to get possession of his property, he went to the Banda Oriental, and opened a store at Mercedes, to support himself.

His troubles had only begun. It was at this time that during the Anglo-French blockade a dispute arose, in consequence of which Colonia, a small town on the coast opposite Buenos Ayres, was fired on by a British ship, and Oribi, Rosa's general, then fighting in the Banda Oriental, declared all French and British subjects in that country to be prisoners of war. It was no mere threat; the order was carried into execution, and in Mercedes alone more than one hundred were arrested, Darrell among them.

These prisoners, mostly French Basques, were collected and ordered to be marched in a body to Durazno, a town sixty leagues north. The *juez de paz*, or justice of the peace, of the place advised the prisoners to take what ready money they had with them, and unfortunately most of them did so. Darrell, however, took only an ounce (£3, 6s.), committing the rest of his property to the care of a friend of his, a citizen of the United States. This was lucky, for scarcely had they set out before the justice of the peace, who had been so kind in offering them his friendly advice, sent men after the party to search them. Justice and peace were both almost strangers in the country at that time, so the poor fellows had to deliver up their purses.

Darrell, who had the advantage of speaking the language fluently, and of being able to associate on friendly terms with the higher class of the natives, was privately forewarned of this by the officer in command, who said that he was very sorry for what was about to be done, that it was beyond his power to stop it, and that he must at least make a show of searching him. The ounce was accordingly delivered up, but afterwards returned. He was at first rather puzzled to explain this forbearance, but understood it when he recognised in the officer a tattered penniless wretch with bare and swollen feet, to whom, while keeping his store in Mercedes, he had a short time before given a pair of boots, telling him to pay for them when he could. One good turn deserves another, and the officer certainly proved himself not ungrateful.

But Darrell scarcely gave him credit for gratitude, when on the second day, as the prisoners were starting from the miserable hut where they had spent the night, this man roughly ordered him to give up his *poncho*, the only thick covering he had.

'Why, would you rob me of my *poncho!*' said Darrell, and the officer hesitated and desisted in his apparently unreasonable demand. But at the next halt the soldiers began to plunder the prisoners, stripping them of every article they possessed. Boots, *ponchos*, *chiripas*, all worth having were seized, and the poor fellows had to continue their march barefoot, and without sufficient clothing even to cover them. Darrell had the vexation of seeing his *poncho*, which the officer had probably intended to save for him, transferred to the back of one of the raggedest soldiers. His watch, too, was taken; luckily they did not find his money. Resistance was useless. The escort was composed of a set of lawless ruffians who plainly would stick at nothing. The day before, a Basque, who had a considerable sum of money, wishing to save some of it, made a bargain with one of the soldiers to give him so much on condition that he should be protected from being searched. Soon afterwards, Darrell saw the two fall behind. He guessed what would be the result, but had no means of preventing it; and his conjectures were right, for in a few minutes the soldier rode up *alone* with the Basco's boots slung over his saddle.

It seems strange that all these outrages should have been allowed by the officer, friendly as he had shown himself; but the fact was, he knew that the wild fellows under his command would have had no hesitation in cutting his throat as well as those of the prisoners, if he attempted to interfere with them in what they considered one of the most legitimate customs of warfare.

On they marched, day after day, suffering every kind of hardship, till at last, one Sunday morning, they arrived at Durazno, and were drawn up in line on the *plaza*. One by one they were called up before an officer, to have their names taken down. Darrell was surprised to find that the captain engaged in this duty was a man whom he had known intimately in Buenos Ayres. The captain, too, stared in mute astonishment, but immediately tried to look unconcerned; recognition might have been dangerous.

Without any explanation he was separated from the other prisoners, and taken in charge by a soldier, who ordered him to follow, and led the way to an empty shed near the gate of the barracks, where Darrell remained for some time alone, shivering with cold, and wondering what was to happen to him. Did this separation from his companions augur good or ill? He scarcely troubled himself about it; his sufferings had made him in a manner indifferent and careless of life. But at the end of half an hour his friend the captain appeared, accompanied by the officer who had commanded the escort, and both, now that they were alone, greeted him in the most cordial manner. They declared their regret at the circumstances which had caused his arrest, and promised to do all in their power to alleviate it. The Commandante of the troops had consented that he was not to live with the other prisoners, but should be quartered in some private house, and be free to go about the town, on parole. The captain then conducted him to his own quarters;

and as they passed through a room in which was a large mirror, he had an opportunity of seeing what a wretched tatterdemalion he looked. But in the officer's room, after the luxury of a bath and a hearty meal, he was comfortably rigged out, and felt ready to forget all his troubles.

Darrell now lived quite at his ease for a time. He soon got acquainted with the principal people of the place; and as he was in high favour with the Commandante, no restraint was laid upon him, though, for the sake of appearance, he made a point of being always present among the prisoners when the roll was called.

At last provisions began to get short; and as the prisoners were likely to suffer, the Commandante, who was a good-natured fellow, resolved to send them to Cerro Largo, a town near the Brazilian frontier, where they would fare better. Remembering the outrages that had been committed on their former journey, they were not very willing to go; but at last all were sent off, except Darrell and three other Englishmen, who also enjoyed the special favour of the Commandante. And before long, these four, beginning to tire of their monotonous life, seeing a prospect of starvation, and hearing that a new detachment of troops, whose commander might not be so friendly, was coming to occupy the town, requested to be sent to Cerro Largo for a change. The Commandante told them he could not spare an escort to send with them, but that they might go alone if they liked, and even gave them a hint that it would be their own fault if they arrived at any destination which was not of their own choice.

Accordingly the four prisoners set out, and as soon as they found themselves in the camp, thoughts of escape were only natural. They resolved to cross over into Brazil, passing by Cerro Largo, however, that they might be unsuspected for the greater part of their journey. A very hard journey they had, as owing to a drought there was no pasture for their horses, and the poor animals got so lean that they could only travel two or three leagues a day; and even then, the riders had to walk half the way and drive the horses before them.

But they contrived to pass Cerro Largo without being questioned, and at last approached the frontier of Brazil. As they drew near the place where they might once more breathe in freedom, the spirits of the tired travellers rose, and they were as merry as holiday makers. They were only half a league from the little river that marked the frontier, and had learned at a *rancho* that the way was clear, all the troops having gone off two days before. There was but one step between them and liberty; already the river was in sight, and the houses and fields on the further bank seemed close at hand, when, alas for their bright hopes, they perceived advancing towards them an officer followed by two tall Indians, armed with lances. There was little time for consultation; the only thing they could do was to go on and face the soldiers as boldly as possible. It was an anxious moment for the little party, unarmed as they were.

'*Buenos dias, señor*,'—'*Buenos dias, amigo*,'—and they had passed by without molestation. Now the unfortunates drew a long breath of relief; but they were to realize the truth of the proverb, 'There's many a slip 'twixt the cup and the lip.' The officer and his men had only gone on a short way, when they wheeled round and began to return at a gallop, shouting to the fugitives to stop. Escape being out of the question, from the state of their horses, the four pulled up.

'Who are you, and where do you come from?' demanded the officer on coming up with them.

'From Durazno, *señor*, and we are going to trade at San Pablo,' they answered.

'Merchants!' said the soldier, looking at their torn clothes and their poverty-stricken horses. 'Impossible! I believe you are rogues. Have you passports?'

What was to be done now? They had only a passport certifying that they were prisoners on their way to Cerro Largo, which was scarcely likely to be of much use to them in the present emergency.

'Can the man read!' was Darrell's first thought; and on the faith that he could not, as a desperate resort, he presented his passport upside down. The officer took the paper and turned it round; it was too plain that he understood its contents perfectly.

'Oh, ho! so you are prisoners on your way to Cerro Largo! How does it come, then, that you are twelve leagues out of the road?'

'We are not acquainted with the country; our horses being so weak, we tried to take a short cut through the camp, and have lost ourselves.'

At this story the officer looked very doubtful. He ordered them to unsaddle.

'Now,' said Darrell in English, 'these fellows will either cut our throats or send us back to Cerro Largo. I for one am going to Brazil.'—

'Agreed,' said the others.

'Watch me; if I get to blows with this man, you tackle the two Indians.'

The latter, dismounted, were leaning over their horses' necks; the officer, laying his hand on Darrell's bridle, repeated his order to unsaddle, and said, 'You are my prisoners.'

THE LAST CHANCE.—*The Pampas*, p. 158.

Suddenly Darrell drew from under his *poncho* an unloaded revolver,—they had no ammunition,—and presenting it at the officer's head, declared he was a dead man, unless he swore on his honour to let them pass over the river. At this the Indians made hostile demonstrations, but they were evidently afraid of the pistol, and the officer, taken aback, ordered them to remain quiet, and gave the promise demanded.

He then turned and galloped off with his men, and the fugitives, suspicious that in spite of his promise he might have gone for assistance to seize them, made as fast as they could for the river bank, and leaving their spent horses there, swam across with some little difficulty, and stood on the Brazilian ground, tired, dripping, almost penniless, but free. They managed to continue their journey to Rio Grande, where they met friends who gave them money, and enabled them to come down by steamer to Monte Video.

So ended Darrell's story, and others were told in the same strain, showing the troubles entailed both upon foreigners and natives by bad government and civil discord. We all agreed such a country would have but a poor chance of prosperity if it were not for the European settlers; and furthermore, that such settlers were likely to be discouraged and scared away if something were not done to diminish the risks and annoyances which they had to undergo. In fact, we took a very cheerful view of our own character and abilities, as contrasted against the background of native incapacity; and this, in spite of grumbling, helped to put us into good humour with ourselves and one another, a frame of mind to be desired at any gathering for social amusement.

The talk turned more and more upon England, which most of us thought of and spoke of as 'home.' It was plain that the colony had no hold on these men's hearts; all their labours were directed to one object, to be able to return home as soon as possible with a competency. I now became a prominent figure in the conversation, for I could tell about the last election, and the underground railway, and the Princess of Wales, and Dickens' newest novel, and various bits of news and scandal which had excited England no later than six months ago. Our American friend rather sneered at this weakness, declaring that the idea of nationalities was almost played out; but even he fired up presently at the barest hint that the 'States' were not the greatest, smartest, freest, and every way most desirable community on earth. He and I had almost quarrelled over this point, but we made friends again before parting, and I afterwards found him to be not half a bad fellow, and learned not to think harshly of people because they don't obey the same government or the same dictionary as oneself. I have since visited the United States, and had reason to know that our cousins' good nature and patriotic zeal are equally 'notorious.'

So the new year approached, but here came a warm dispute as to when it really did begin. Every watch in the party showed a divergence of at least ten minutes, and Darrell added to our perplexity by suggesting that we might perhaps be mistaking the day as well as the hour,—an occurrence far from uncommon in regions remote from newspapers and church clocks. This was too bad to be believed; so, on the motion of one of the Simpsons, we agreed to make it twelve o'clock of the 31st of December, and hailed the new year with three loud cheers and a general shaking of hands and exchanging of good wishes all round.

After this the party broke up, at what, for the Pampas, was an extraordinarily late and dissipated hour. When the rest had gone, we three, having not so far to ride, stayed a little longer with the Simpsons. We sat smoking in the dark round the dying embers, and our talk grew more quiet and thoughtful, as the minds of these voluntary exiles went back to Christmas scenes of the past, and old associations began to exercise their softening influence. By and by, in a pause of conversation, Fred Simpson's fine voice struck up the good old carol—

> 'God rest you, honest gentlemen,
> Let nothing you dismay.'

This led to one or two other Christmas songs and hymns; and then, as if the words familiar from childhood had laid a spell on our tongues, our talk took a sober tone, less usual in this rough life, and we touched not irreverently on things which are perhaps too much spoken of and too little felt in the churches and chapels of civilisation. Men who are much alone on a vast wilderness, and daily struggling hand to hand with the forces of nature, must be dull indeed, if they never think of life's mysterious problems. They see the works of the Lord as surely as those who go down into deep waters, and their solitary thoughts will often put life into old words and songs that may have once seemed hard, dry commonplaces, as well as call back something of the mingled awe and trust with which childhood's pure eyes first looked on the wonders of the universe. His memories of home are the religion of the wanderer, and these memories now opened our hearts and drew forth words that at other seasons would perhaps have been left unspoken.

About one o'clock, we, too, spoke of going. The

Simpsons pressed us to stay all night, but we thought it best to return home. Afterwards we had good reason to remember this. We said good night to our friendly hosts, and galloped off in the moonlight, little dreaming what should be our next visit to 'Belvoir Castle.'

'Good fellows the Simpsons are!' we all declared, as we rode home, stumbling here and there upon *biscacho* or armadillo holes, but seeing no sign of more serious danger upon the wide plain that all round us lay white and silent under the moon.

CHAPTER IX.

A NEW YEAR'S DAY.

NEXT morning, after our unwonted dissipation, we were all late of getting up; and when we came outside we found our *peons*, cigarette in mouth, engaged in looking hard at a faint cloud which rose above the level plain in the direction of the Simpsons' *estancia*.

'Is that smoke?' asked Desmond; and we gathered together to examine it.

By the aid of a field-glass, which was one of the treasures I had brought with me, we made out that it was, beyond doubt, a pillar of smoke, and of such a size that it must be caused by no ordinary fire. What could be the matter?

'*Quien sabe?*' replied the *peons*, shrugging their shoulders and rolling fresh cigarettes.

But we were not so easily satisfied. This might be the beginning of a camp-fire, which, as the wind was in our quarter, would be upon us in a very short time; and we had almost begun to burn a space on one side of the *estancia*, where, the pasture being long and dry, the flames might have endangered the house. But from this anxiety we were soon set free. We watched the smoke for more than half an hour, during which it dwindled away, till we could barely make it out through the field-glass. Then we began to fear that some disaster must have fallen on our friends, and all breakfast-time we spoke of sending over to see what had happened. Somehow, even then a vague sense of dread seemed to have taken hold of us; and though we scarcely cared to do more than hint at our apprehensions, each one of us showed a strange reluctance to be the first to learn the truth. But we tried to hope that it was only a shed which had accidentally taken fire.

After breakfast a man rode up with letters from the post-office at Villa Grande. We, and a few other settlers in the neighbourhood, had arranged to have our letters sent round by a special messenger, as otherwise we only got them when we could call or send for them, and the post was very irregular. Even in this way, our letters took almost as long coming from Buenos Ayres, as they did on the voyage from England to the capital.

'De post! de post!' shouted Senecio, who had

learned so much of English, and was always eager to make this announcement, knowing that it never failed to put all his masters into a most good-humoured state of expectancy, in which his own peccadillos were sure to be forgotten. To-day we were especially satisfied to see our private postman, as he must just have come from the Simpsons' *estancia*, and would bring us news of how they were.

Desmond and I met this messenger outside of the *corral;* and when we took the letters from him, we could not help noticing that he looked frightened and confused, while the state of his horse showed that he had ridden the last few miles at a furious pace. The first thing we asked him was if he knew anything about the Simpsons ; and instead of answering, he handed us a packet of letters, among them two addressed to our neighbours.

'Speak out, man. What's the matter?' said Desmond ; then, seeing that the *gaucho* only stared at him, he hurriedly repeated his question in Spanish.

But it is not easy to make a *gaucho* speak out, especially when he is in such a state of trepidation as our man evidently was; and though we saw plainly, from his manner, that something serious had happened, we had to cross-examine him for some time before he could tell us what he had seen ; and even then, we felt sure that he had not told us all. Had he been to the Simpsons'? Yes—but the house was burned—everything. How? He did not know—he thought the Indians had been there. And the masters of the *estancia?* He had seen no one; he had ridden away at once. But, on being pressed, he confessed that there was something in the ditch—something which he did not like to examine; he would rather say no more; he advised us to keep at home, and look after ourselves; he would go no farther that day. This was all we could get from him, but it was enough to quicken our worst fears on our friends' behalf, as well as to warn us that we must neglect no precautions to provide for our own safety.

'Good heavens! the Indians must be out again; and these poor fellows were all alone last night, after we left them.'

'Perhaps they have been carried off.'

'*Perhaps—*'

This was the only occasion, during my stay in camp, on which letters from home were not welcomed with joy. Generally, each man would seize upon his little budget with a shout of triumph; and as soon as his occupation was over, and he could be secure of an uninterrupted spell of leisure, would retire to some quiet corner, and there, sitting in his shirt sleeves, would pore over the precious pages with such avidity, that he would be actually sorry to learn that dinner was ready. But to-day we had no heart to do more than tear open the envelopes, and by a hasty glance at the contents, assure ourselves that all was well at home; and I, for one, could not bear to look at the two letters addressed to the poor fellows with whom we had spent last evening so pleasantly, but whom we feared we might never see again.

Desmond and the rest of us at once set about preparing for a possible attack; though we agreed that if the Indians were coming our way, we should probably have seen them by this time. Jim and one of the *peons* were sent to drive in the horses; the sheep were left to take their chance, as these marauders seldom used to drive off animals which would impede their rapid flight. In more recent raids, I am told that, attacking in greater numbers and with more daring, they have carried away whatever they could get.

The messenger, who had brought so bad news, begged hard to be allowed to stay with us; but such a coward as he appeared to be would be of no use in our small garrison, so he was sent off on a fresh horse to Monte Bustos. Here were two stations belonging, one to some Englishmen, the other to a German; all of them, except one, had been among the guests of the previous evening; and as their camp lay farther back from the frontier of civilisation, on which we formed, as it were, an extreme outpost, we knew that they would not hesitate to come to our help. For ourselves, anxious as we were to learn the fate of our friends, we durst not leave the station unprotected, and all forenoon we kept watch on the roof of the house, sweeping the camp with our fieldglasses, and especially watching the quarter from which the Indians might be expected to come. But we could see no signs of them, though once we were for a minute deceived by a flock of ostriches scudding along between us and the edge of the horizon.

Everything was ready for the enemy if they should come; the firearms were all loaded; a rude line of defence was hastily constructed, of which the hut formed the citadel, while a circle was completed by our cart, a few old boxes, and some posts which we luckily had saved from those for the *corral*, though we had often been tempted to use them for firewood, logs of wood of any size being very valuable in our treeless neighbourhood. These we now fixed in the ground at short intervals, and stretched hides between them. Even our wheelbarrow was used in the construction of the barricade, and our furniture, down to the very door taken off its hinges, was pressed into the service. In the hut itself we were prepared to put the best horses, if the worst came to the worst; we should like to have gathered them all into our enclosure, but were afraid that, getting frightened, they might break down the defences as soon as the fighting began.

'If the devils would only come now!' exclaimed Desmond, a dozen times at least; and each of us shared his feelings.

'And if they do come, they shan't all go away again,' quoth Eckford grimly.

In the afternoon we felt that we could no longer endure this uncertainty, and it was agreed that, while the rest kept guard at home, Desmond, one of the *peons*, and I, should ride over to our neighbours' station.

'I don't think there is any chance of them now,' said Bob Eckford. 'Some of these other fellows will be turning up soon. In the meanwhile you may leave me alone, and I'll take my chance.'

He didn't count the *peons;* Senecio was worth less than nothing, even to load the firearms, for in his agitation he had already pulled the trigger of a rifle he was dealing with, and might have shot one of us, if he had not previously been considerate enough to put the ball in before the powder.

We set off at full speed, and half an hour's gallop brought us in sight of the place which yesterday had been a little oasis of civilisation in this desert, but which we soon saw to be now nothing but a heap of blackened ruins. We spurred on our horses, but in our hearts we feared to arrive at that abode of desolation.

Not a sound greeted our approach; but a few *carranchas*, with their great hooked bills, rose scared from the ruins, and descended into the grass a little way off, as if only waiting till we should be gone to return upon their prey. I did not know what was the nature of these ominous birds, but I guessed when I looked at Desmond, and saw how he set his lips tight together. The only other sign of life about the spot was a couple of young lambs who were playing beside the remains of some sheep, which seemed to have been hurriedly slaughtered near the house. By this time we were close to it, and Desmond pulled up, and cried—

'What's that in the ditch?'

I did not need to look. I knew well what it must be. We rode up and saw lying before us the bodies of our friends, stripped, horribly mutilated, and already so discoloured and torn by the birds of prey as to be scarcely recognisable. All round about, the torn and broken fragments of such of their belongings as had escaped the fire, and had not seemed worth carrying off, bore witness to the savage fury of the murderers.

I can never forget that sight. These were the men with whom we had passed the last evening so jovially; their jests and laughter came rushing back upon us at this moment with painful distinctness; we remembered how one of them had mirthfully spoken of seeing strangers at the bottom of his tea-cup, little knowing, poor fellows, what strangers were soon to be upon them; then we thought of these unopened letters which we carried with us, and recalled again how full of life and hope the men had been, and how they talked of the successful year they had reason to expect, and reckoned up the time which would enable them to return home as rich men, with all the glee of schoolboys looking forward to the holidays. It seemed only an hour ago that we parted with them in such good spirits, and they had pressed our hands so warmly, wishing us a happy new year, and promising that we should all see each other again before many days were gone; and now, horror-struck and silent, we stood looking down upon—we could not bear it. We turned away together, as if moved by one will. We knew that the same thoughts were passing through our minds, but we durst not trust ourselves to speak.

The *peon*, after one glance at the corpses, had been searching about the ruins, and presently he came back with another native whom we at once recognised as having been in the Simpsons' service. This man slunk up in a way that made us suspect him of treachery; but on being questioned he told a tale which we had no means of contradicting, and which, I daresay, was not far from the truth. His own life, he said, he only owed to the intervention of one of his own countrymen among the Indian band, who contrived to let him slip away, and advised him to hide himself in the long grass. The other natives had been taken away as prisoners, and the two European servants were, luckily for themselves, absent at Villa Grande, where they had been sent to be out of the way of the party. This may sound strange, but of course a servant out there is too proud to be a flunkey.

If the account of the *peon* was to be relied upon, the Indians, some hundreds strong,—though that was probably an exaggeration,—had surprised them before daybreak. Roused by the trampling of the horses, the Englishmen had just time to get into their fort, while their native attendants had at once attempted to fly. The Indians then called out that if the *señors* would surrender and give up all they had, their lives would be spared. But the Simpsons were not the men to give in while there was any chance of defending themselves; they had mercilessly chaffed Bob Eckford and me about our late adventure; and now they were well armed and trusted to the strength of their fort, far more than to the good faith of their assailants. They answered the Indians' proposal by firing on them, as, dismounted, they were swarming over the ditch, but it was probably too dark to see if the shots took effect. Unfortunately they had left several little heaps of earth standing about the enclosure, and behind the shelter of these we could imagine that the Indians had been able to creep close up to the fort without exposing themselves. Our poor friends had made a still more serious oversight. The thatched roof had been covered with mud to make it fire-proof, but at the eaves little bunches of cane had been left uncovered. By one of the strange chances which are perhaps even more common in real life than in fiction, some of their guests of the day before, while inspecting the fortification, had pointed out the danger of this, and the elder brother had confessed that it was a weak point, and carelessly said that he would see to it as soon as he had time. The Indians had probably noticed this, and took advantage of it. Among the other articles left behind in the shed, that they had obtained possession of, was a jar of oil. In this they dipped bunches of grass, and, fastening them to the points of their long spears, pushed them against the exposed corners of the thatch. The dry canes were in a blaze in an instant, and the Englishmen found themselves in danger from this new and terrible enemy. They tried to remain inside, and kept firing as often as they got a chance; but the heat and the smoke nearly suffocated them, and at last, unable to bear it longer, they made a rush out and were instantly surrounded and butchered. The Indians then proceeded to make a complete wreck of the place, acting like madmen in their fury of destruction; and when the sun rose the work was done, and the dead bodies having been flung into the ditch, the savage crew rode away southwards.

Such was the tale to which we now listened, supplying its imperfections by very obvious guesses at the facts,—a tale all the more disheartening, because it represented the Indians as showing a degree of boldness and cunning for which we had not given them credit, and warned us that this was perhaps not the last time we might be present at a similar scene. They even appeared to have had firearms; at all events, bullet marks were found on the bodies of their victims, though we could not be sure that these were not made after death by their own weapons, which were missing. If any of the Indians were killed, the bodies had been removed by their comrades. It is scarcely likely that two well-armed Englishmen would have been overpowered without a deadly resistance.

This was indeed a sorrowful New Year's Day for us. While the *peons* were digging a shallow grave, Desmond and I searched among the fragments of books and furniture which were strewn about. Most of the things were destroyed, but we picked up the poor fellows' photographic album, which of course we carefully put away, and also a copy of Dickens' *Cricket on the Hearth*, that Eckford had lent them not long before. Besides, we found the torn leaves of a prayer-book of the Church of England, and Desmond attempted to read part of the burial service over the bodies, when we had laid them reverently in the ground. But his voice trembled, and he handed the leaf to me. I tried to go on, but I, too, broke down; so we silently filled up the grave, and with no other rite than a last look at the little mound of freshly dug earth, red in the light of the setting sun, we turned away and left our friends to sleep in peace in that solitary plain, which one day shall be full of life and labour, and where busy feet shall tread over their bones, and busy minds shall plan schemes for wealth and pleasure, thinking little how the foundations of this new civilisation were laid.

Desmond rode off at once to Villa Grande to inform the Commandante of what had happened, and, if possible, to rouse him to action. I returned home, where I found that we need be in no dread of Indians, as some half-dozen of our neighbours had assembled, and were eager to avenge the shocking death of the Simpsons, who had been such great favourites with all. But we could do nothing till we had intelligence as to the whereabouts of the enemy, and the assistance we could expect from the authorities.

As the most literary member of the party, I was appointed to open and answer the two letters addressed to the dead men. I never had such a hard task in my life. One of them was from the Simpsons' agent in Buenos Ayres; the other was dated from a Gloucestershire parsonage, and written by a lady who signed herself 'Nelly,'—a sister, I supposed, or perhaps a sweetheart, but of course I did not read it through. For two hours I tried to write a note that might go back with it, and explain why these loving lines had never reached the eye of him for whom they had been intended But when I thought of my message creeping over sea and land on its sorrowful mission, and of the bright English household which at length, some morning, it would reach, to fill with misery and darkness, and of the eagerness with which that happy girl would snatch at this envelope from a far land, and of the cold doubt which would fall upon her heart as she saw the strange handwriting, and of the cry of woe which my news would wring from her when she opened and read, I could not do it. I enclosed both letters to the agent, telling him briefly of the calamity, and asking him to inform the relatives at home. It was moral cowardice on my part, and I repented of it afterwards, and tried to make up for it by collecting and taking home to the family all the relics of their lost ones which we could find.

Next morning Desmond came back, with news that the Commandante had promised to be with us later in the day, and bring a force which should effectually overawe the Indians. We waited for him all day in vain. On the day after, however, he arrived at the head of a body of ferocious-looking horsemen, armed to the teeth with miscellaneous weapons, terrible to behold, but not otherwise very deadly. Only two or three had firearms, and seemed much more afraid of them than any one else was likely to be. We spent all the day in scouring about the camp and smoking cigarettes, and the native militia loudly expressed their desire to meet the marauders, all the more loudly, when we could find no signs of them anywhere. Of course, the Indians had gone home after their successful raid ; and when we had had enough of our unsuccessful search, we went home also. But not—I refer to the English and German settlers—without concerting among ourselves a plan by which we should be able to unite for common defence, if ever the Indians showed themselves in the neighbourhood again.

The settlers had almost given up hope of help from the authorities, to whom they had applied again and again for an efficient guard of the frontier. A wise Government would, of course, have been zealous to protect men who were laboriously adding to the area of the country's prosperity, and step by step conquering for civilisation those vast plains that as yet only in name were part of the State. But governments are not always wise, especially South American governments. And at this time the Argentine States were engaged in the desperate war roused by the ambition of Lopez, the Dictator of Paraguay, and could not spare troops for any other purpose till it was ended. So the foreign settlers had nothing for it but to protect themselves, which, indeed, they were better able to do than the authorities.

CHAPTER X.

LIFE ON THE CAMP.

WHEN I awake now at, let us say, eight o'clock on a January morning of the present year, I expect to be allowed a comfortable little snooze, after looking out to see what sort of a day it is, and, when I have made up my mind about getting up, to find my bath ready, my clothes brushed, my dressing-case open; then, having made a deliberate toilet, I come down to a neatly ordered room, a cheerful fire, 'bright laid breakfast,' and the other little luxuries of civilised and respectable society. But if ever I should be inclined to feel annoyed that my fire has not burned up, that the newspaper has not come, that the coffee is cold,—in short, that somebody has not been duly caring for my comfort,—I might console myself by thinking of the way we used to live on the Pampas.

There, in the short twilight, one was awakened by a horse neighing for his breakfast, and jumped up and looked out to see the sun's rim peeping over the plain. No time was spent in dozing. Whoever woke first would give a shout and a shake to his companions, and putting on a single garment, would be off to the well to bring a bucket of water. Presently the others would emerge, more or less undressed, and the bucket would serve us all to perform our ablutions in the open air. As the wintry month of *May* drew on, there would perhaps be a touch of fog or frost to remind us of home, but in the midsummer weather of January the scene was always beautiful, the air fresh and cool. Somebody would bring out the blankets and hang them up in the sun; somebody else would go to rouse up the *peons*, who slept in the open air at the back of the hut. Then one of them would go off, rubbing his eyes, to seek materials for a fire, and the other would appear on the roof, scanning the horizon to see in which direction the horses had gone through the night. The fire lighted, some one got breakfast ready for himself and the rest. Mutton and biscuit, as usual; the coffee was boiled in a kettle, and a cinder dropped in to make it settle. Another task was hunting for Senecio, who used to select all sorts of out-of-the-way holes and corners for his sleeping-place, that he might have as long a nap as he could.

In about half an hour the *peon* who had gone in

search of the horses would return, driving the whole troop before him at a hard trot, the bell mare in front. They were penned up in the *corral*, those required for the day picked out and tied up; the others let go. We had a cow, too, which the other *peon* was milking meanwhile, after which he would look after the bullocks for the cart.

The sun is now high, and the sheep are let out, or rather are forced out, though, if we wished them to stay in, they would be doing their best to break through the fence—such is the perverse disposition of the animal. As soon as they are outside of the *corral*, some obstinate old ewe, which has been the last to show signs of moving, turns frisky and makes for the unfinished garden fence, leading all the rest of the flock after her into mischief. This affords us a little exercise both of legs and lungs, and at last we get them headed and sent off in a right direction, and return to our breakfast as we see them settling down to theirs. As soon as breakfast is over, one of us, on this duty for the day, rides after them to spend a lonely morning. The others stay at home, put up fences, dig ditches, work in the garden, stir up the *peons*, or in some other way make themselves useful, and get prodigious appetites for dinner.

The man with the sheep has a dreary job of it.

Perhaps the provoking flock pretend to settle down, and delude him into taking out a book and beginning to read. But, so sure as he has just got to an interesting paragraph, they are taken with a restless fit, and the whole flock, young and old, set off at a trot, with the apparent intention of exploring the pastures of some distant part of the country, quite regardless of the shepherd's convenience. Right glad he is when the shortening shadow of his horse announces that noon is at hand, and, unless his woolly charge are more than ordinarily troublesome, he may gallop home for dinner. If he don't appear, a gun will perhaps be fired, by way of dinner-bell; on some camps they hoisted a flag as a signal.

We always dined—we called it dinner, at least—punctually at twelve, that is, when the building ceased to throw any shade; the sun was our clock, and often we thought him behind. We had watches, but we often forgot to wind them up, and did not trust them much, though, if we compared them with other men's watches, there was seldom more than an hour's difference. Dinner finished, we would take a pipe and perhaps read a book, or, as a great treat, a newspaper two months old.

But the heat is terrible; the *peons* are already taking their *siesta* outside, and soon we too go to sleep, as well as the flies will let us, which at this time of the year are a veritable plague. If at this hour any one were to enter our humble abode, he would see three gentlemen in various stages of undress, stretched out on the floor or on benches, each with a book in his hand, but each slumbering more or less soundly. Watch Eckford's face. Half a dozen flies are crawling about his lips, another party are amusing themselves on his eyes, a numerous band are playing hide-and-seek in his ears, and three or four adventurous ones are tickling the point of his nose. These last exhaust his patience; and after winking and twitching convulsively, he half starts up, hits himself a blow on the nose, and with an angry grunt wheels round with his face to the wall. Desmond has folded his arms doggedly over his face, and snores resolutely in defiance of the insects. I am turning and twisting like an eel, not yet accustomed to these little tormentors, but by and by the heat gets the best of it, and for an hour I forget all troubles, great and small.

About three we wake up, yawning and heavy-eyed, and go once more about our tasks. The man who is looking after the sheep rides back to the spot where in the meantime they have been taking their *siesta*, lying by the side of a *laguna*, or beneath some scrubby bushes, or, if they can do no better, standing in groups of some half a dozen, with their heads together, so as to try and get into each other's shadow. Shade, shade, that is what all nature is sighing for in our part of the world, while you are running off to Brighton or Nice, hunting for a few beams of the sunshine which we could so well spare.

The afternoon would wear on to a more pleasant hour when the air grew cooler, the sunlight more mellow, and the thin patches of shadow lengthening out, gave notice that it was time to knock off work. Then perhaps we met at the *laguna* for a bathe in its least slimy puddle,—a delicious luxury, tempered by the fear of coming out with a leech or two sticking to one's legs, or by the sight of a brown and white snake that had crept into the water to regale itself on a frog. Thus refreshed, we would saunter home to our evening meal. But first the sheep had to be penned up in the *corral*, the horses fed and turned out, *yerba* and sugar to be served out to the *peons*, who would exhaust their ingenuity to work an extra share out of the good-nature of the storekeeper, and then we might stand by the door, looking at the soft crimson glow of the sunset sky, broken only by a flock of geese sailing southwards, or be still more surely tempted by these too short minutes of twilight,

> 'When the quiet-coloured end of evening smiles
> Miles and miles.'

But soon the darkness draws round, and sentiment gives place to appetite; and by the light of a tallow candle or a small paraffin lamp, we sit down to a hearty repast, which may be called dinner or tea or supper. As soon as it is over, pipes are lit, and if there is a moon, we loaf outside for an hour or two; but, as a rule, between nine and ten we are ready for bed.

Our beds were not ready for us, however, till we had made them,—an operation of no small labour, which was performed in the following way. We had one proper bed, and a rickety affair it was. For the framework of the others two benches were put together, also two or three boxes, pieces of wood being shoved in beneath the latter to make them stand level. When a visitor was sleeping with us, we had to make up another bed, into the composition of which our wheelbarrow entered largely; but if possible we managed without it, and I cannot say that it was comfortable. Two doors, belonging to the extra room which had not yet got built, were then laid on these erections, and on the top a few sheepskins were arranged, waterproof coats were spread out to serve as sheets, and the covering would consist of a rug, a coat or two, a saddle-cloth, or any other convenient article. Trousers, and garments of that sort, not being of much value as blankets, were rolled up to be used as pillows. The only thing that remained to be done was to toss up for who should have *the* bed, which was sumptuously furnished with real blankets, but in other respects was little more luxurious than those I have described. The lucky winner at once turned in to secure possession; the other two made themselves as comfortable as they could, and soon we were all fast asleep.

Not always. Perhaps I would lie awake till midnight; and to my unaccustomed ears, every stir in the solitude around us would seem cause of alarm, till at last I would make sure the Indians were about, and would call out to the other two:

'Desmond, are you asleep?'

'H'm!' a little grunt from Desmond, and a long snore from Bob Eckford.

'I say, Desmond' (*earnestly*).

'What's the matter with you?' (*sleepily*).

'I wonder what these dogs can be barking at?' (*suspiciously*).

'Oh, nothing! Don't bother a fellow' (*sulkily*).

'But I'm sure there's some one about, Desmond. Just listen!' (The dogs bark louder; Bob's snoring rises above all.)

'I wish somebody would hang the brutes,' growls Desmond. 'I think we had better get up and see what's the matter.'

'Should we?' (Silence for a minute.) 'I say, Desmond, shall we get up, and take a look about?' (*persuasively*).

'Oh! get up? Yes' (*feebly*). Neither of us move.

'Will you get up if I do? Come on, man' (*encouragingly*).

Desmond, with sudden energy — 'Very well.' (Flings off his bed-clothes and sits up, yawning.) ' Look sharp, then!'

He springs out of bed, I follow his example, the dogs barking more and more furiously; and presently two figures in white, barefoot, revolver in hand, glide forth and lie down on the ground, shivering and peering into the darkness, but see nothing. The dogs at once stop barking, run up and wag their tails in a convivial manner. Now nothing is to be heard but Bob's steady snoring within, unless, as I once did in these circumstances, I let off my revolver by accident, and nearly shot away my great toe.

Desmond (after a minute) — 'There's nothing the matter. Oh, how cold it is!'

Myself — 'Isn't it!' (*shuddering*).

Here Jim appears, roused from his bed beneath the bullock cart. On being informed of the cause of our restlessness, he mutters a few uncomplimentary remarks, meant partly for us, and partly for the dogs; to the latter he administers a few kicks, not having taken off his boots to go to bed, or in fact any article of clothing, except his hat. We listen again; nothing to be heard.

All—'Confound these dogs! let us go to bed again.'

The figures glide noiselessly back, the revolvers are put away, the dogs begin again, and after a few strong remarks about their stupidity, we get to sleep, the night air bath having cooled my excited fancy.

This is a *fair* specimen of five days out of six of our camp-life. I didn't mean to make a pun in the above sentence, but I was going to say that the weather sometimes interfered to break the monotony. Wet days, much as they are desired when the grass is burned up by weeks of heat, bring no little inconvenience to the settler who cannot yet afford to have a good house over his head. My visit was mainly in the fine weather, when rain is not frequent; but we had one or two thoroughly drenching days, which have left a dismal enough picture in my memory.

Here we are staying at home in intense discomfort, almost in positive wretchedness; servants and all crowded into our one room, for on such a day you have scarcely the heart to keep a dog out of doors. A chill wind is driving a deluge of rain before it, and now and then, as a variation, a shower of thick sleet. Outside, everything is turned into mud and water; inside, we lie and sit about, yawning and listening to the rain as it rattles loudly on the roof, and shifting our places as here and there it finds its way through a chink, and comes dripping down on the damp ground. We light the stove, but the wind being from the south, the smoke and flames go the wrong way; the chimney has been blown down during the night. We open the door, and the wind rushes in strong enough to set all the contents of the room in motion; we shut it, and are choked and blinded in five minutes. We have to make the best of a cold, comfortless meal. We can settle to no employment; every look out of doors drives us to despair; we can only think of the mischief the storm is doing. The horses are not to be seen; the bullocks have been driven away before the storm to *Quien sabe* where; the sheep are nearly stiff with cold, yet we dare not let them out of the *corral*. Some manage to break out by themselves, and we get soaked to the skin while chasing them in again. We are all cross and tired. Perhaps one of us has a cold in his head. Can you imagine a scene of greater misery? 'What fools we were to leave home!' is now the general declaration.

Somehow or other the blustering hours pass away, and at last the dreary twilight gives place to pitch darkness. The wind blows wilder, the rain falls heavier than ever. Now, however, strange to say, our spirits began to rise. We are tired of moping; we pluck up courage and defy the storm, thinking how much worse it would be if we were on the open plain. Though to-morrow the horses will be miles away, though a lot of the sheep will be dead of cold, sufficient for the day is the evil thereof; we won't think of such things to-night. The lamp is lit, and the stove, in spite of the smoke. We manage to make a comfortable tea. Eckford brings out his concertina. Desmond and I sit down to backgammon. The *peons* drink *maté* and doze in a corner. Senecio pervades the room, grinning; his cheerfulness, at least, has been uninterrupted. Shall we bold Britons, then, not raise a triumphant chorus, and challenge the storm-fiend to do his worst, in the inspiring strains of 'The Bay of Biscay, O!' or 'The British Grenadiers'? At last, reminding one another how much good this rain will do in the end, we go to bed, and sleep soundly, lulled by the roaring of the storm.

When Sunday came, we never failed to keep it with due respect. Only absolutely necessary work was done; we dressed more carefully than usual, at least to the extent of a paper collar; even Jim wore his best knife. The worst of it was, that as it was difficult to keep count of our uneventful days, we were not always sure as to which was Sunday. One of our friends had a wicked tale against us, that, riding over one *Tuesday* to see if we could lend him an axe, he found us all sitting idle in our best things, looking very serious or reading good books.

I am afraid we generally began the day by lying in bed a little longer than ordinary. And, as a usual thing, we tried to get up a rather better dinner, in the preparation of which we would all take part. After dinner we would read, or saunter about, or write letters home; a still more favourite occupation was looking over our photographic albums and talking about one another's sisters. Eckford used to make most praiseworthy efforts to teach Senecio to read out of a Spanish Testament; but whether the fault was with the teacher or the learner, very little progress was made. In the evenings we would sometimes fill our stove with maize cobs, and sit round the fine glossy glow which they threw out, talking or thinking—nearly always of home.

During the latter part of my stay, an arrangement was made by which a clergyman came once a month from Rosario, and held a service in our little hut, which on such occasions was as full as it could hold. All the morning, men could be seen coming across the camp in knots of two or three, and gathering into groups round our door. We were hard put to it for pews; but what with benches and boxes, we could do with a congregation of from twenty to thirty, which was the average number. The clergyman, who brought his surplice with him, and put it on in the tent, was boxed up behind a table placed across one corner of the room, with a pile of books covered by a blanket for reading-desk. Rough as such arrangements were, the little congregation was always serious and attentive. These services were highly valued by all English settlers, if not for their own sake, at least for the opportunity they gave our countrymen of meeting together. I should think there was no parish in the world where the clergyman was such a welcome visitor.

Visitors were, of course, our main sources of excitement. In some stations near the towns, 'loafers' abound rather too much, and keep dropping in so often, especially at meal times, that it is made a point of etiquette that a guest shall take his share of whatever work may be going; you can't turn a man away from your bed and board, but you can at least insist on him not being idle at your expense. This rule was only relaxed in the case of one or two comic individuals, who might be called jesters by profession, for they made their living apparently by going about the camp, where they were almost everywhere welcomed on account of their amusing qualities, and most frequented the houses where they had the easiest time of it.

A good story was told of an Oxford man, who came out with the professed view of writing a book about the Pampas. Like some other authors, he was very lazy, and, whatever his writings might be, his conversation was dull; in fact, he scarcely concealed that he could not bring his great mind down to the level of the *estancieros*, whose talk was of wool and mutton. He stayed, however, for three weeks at one place, mooning about and smoking, till the owner got tired of him, and resolved to make him work at something. But the literary character made a mess of every job entrusted to him, and at last his host in disgust set him to churn some *sour milk*. Languidly the gentleman got to work, reading a novel all the time; and when the rest of the party came back to dinner, they found he had given it up in despair.

'It *won't* come,' he said; 'and I have nearly made a skeleton of myself, trying.'

There was a great laugh at his expense, and he was so annoyed when he understood what a trick had been played on him, that next day he was off, and, so far as I know, his book has not yet appeared. No doubt it would have been very much more elegant and instructive than the present volume.

But we lived so far out of the way, that visitors were rare, and we were always glad to see one, and eager to make much of him. The greatest bore alive, I believe, might have come to stay with us, and made sure of being warmly received, and treated to the fatted calf; for we were apt to grow tired of each other's talk, and to hear a new voice was quite a relief. We could all say, with Shakespeare, of this kind of life: 'Truly, in respect of itself, it is a good life; but in respect that it is a shepherd's life, it is naught. In respect that it is solitary, I like it very well; but in respect that it is private, it is a very vile life. Now, in respect that it is in the fields, it pleaseth me well; but in respect that it is not in the court, it is tedious'—sometimes.

Then, of course, our occupations were occasionally varied by such scenes as I have already spoken of, marking, parting or shearing animals, either at our own or at another station. Or here, for instance, one morning we have a *manada* of wild mares driven into the *corral*, and a *tropero*, cigarette in mouth, is riding about inspecting them with critical eye. This *tropero* is a man who travels about collecting useless cattle and horses, which, if fit for nothing else, he drives into the *saladeros*, or slaughtering-houses on the rivers, to be killed for their hides and tallow. Mares are for this purpose kept wild in *manadas* or herds, but the man who was seen riding on a mare in this country would be unmercifully laughed at—why, I cannot say. So the herd have been brought in, and are being penned up into a corner by the natives, who all the while keep shouting and wheeling lassos over their heads, ready to be launched at the first one that may try to escape. The poor mares, dreading the resistless weapon, become mad with fright and fury, and dash about frantically, trying perhaps to clear the palisade, but in vain, while the *tropero* is calculating whether he can afford to give twenty-five reals apiece for those pointed out to him, which the owner wishes to get rid of.

A fine stallion is being bargained for; suddenly, as if guessing that his fate is even now decided, he breaks from the rest, and tears down the narrow lane left between the men and the paling. In a moment three lassos are hurled after him; two are badly thrown; the third is round his head. He struggles, rears, and makes one tremendous bound at the gate, only succeeding, however, in breaking one of the heavy bars, and falling on his back in the effort. He rolls round—again he rises —he plunges forward; the man holding the lasso, with his body thrown back, and his feet planted firmly on the ground, lets himself be dragged along for a few yards. The *tropero* snatches the cord from his hand, and turns his well-trained horse to follow the doomed animal, which is allowed to make one more race half across the *corral*, then with a skilful twist thrown heavily to the ground. This time he does not rise; a second lasso is round his legs, and a *peon* is holding down his head, while another, unsheathing his long, sharp knife, makes a slit in the inside of both ears. He is then drawn into the next *corral*, and turned loose. The rest submit more quietly; but when the *tropero* is ready to set out with his new acquisitions, it will be as much as all the men about the place can do to drive them away from the familiar neighbourhood. This slitting of the ears seems cruel, but it is said to be the only way of taming horses down to be driven. Cruelty to animals is unfortunately only too common in that country. I once went to one of these great slaughter-houses, where I actually saw some lads amusing themselves by hacking at a half-dead cow with their knives. When I called the attention of one of the men about the place to this horrible barbarity, he only shrugged his shoulders and walked on, looking rather surprised at my thinking it worth while to take notice of such a trifle.

One amusement of ours was so much a matter of course, that I had almost forgot to mention it. We had plenty of shooting; indeed, we were too often tempted to neglect our work in this way, and waste our powder as well as our time; for when we were at it, we would sometimes shoot in an hour or two more than we could eat for a week. Herds of deer and South American ostriches were constantly wandering about within sight; and though they were shy of coming near the house, we stalked them from our ditch, or brought them suddenly down with a rifle shot from the roof. One very effectual way of getting near the ostriches was to go out into the open camp, and lie down, putting a rug over your heels, and kicking it violently in the air, till you had excited their attention. Then these birds, who are the most inquisitive as well as the most stupid creatures, would come scudding up to the number of perhaps twenty or thirty, and keep walking round you, and peering at the strange sight till you were ready to take a right and left shot at them with your revolver. And even when one fell, the rest would run up to see what was the matter with it, and you could have as many as you pleased for the trouble of shooting straight into them. But they were not very good for eating; their flesh was like tough, stringy beef with a gamey flavour. There were also a kind of small partridges, as stupid as the ostriches, which we scarcely took the trouble to shoot; they would allow a cunning native, going round in a circle, and coming always nearer, to noose them in a loop at the end of a cane. Besides, we had often flocks of wild-fowl, white swans with black necks, and flamingoes with their pink breasts, so beautiful that it went to one's heart to kill them. They were generally to be found in the evening by the *laguna*, and it was a pretty sight to see a flock of them rising like a crimson cloud in the light of the setting sun. Wild ducks, too, of several kinds, often paid us a visit. I remember, one day, Desmond and I were shooting them in the *laguna*, up to our knees in water; and the sport grew so exciting, that when my cousin ran out of paper, he actually tore up a part of his *new* flannel shirt for wadding.

One other animal I must not omit to mention. Few 'new chums' escaped an unpleasant experience on first meeting it. The confiding youth would see a pretty little white and black creature like a squirrel looking inoffensively at him not far off. Keeping his rifle ready, he would approach cautiously in the hope of catching it alive, and when he was close at hand—*it was a skunk*. After that, the only thing to do with one's clothes was to hang them up in the open air for a month or two, as far from the house as possible.

I have said nothing about our costume, in which, as may be imagined, we consulted mainly our own taste and convenience. In the hot weather Desmond generally wore at home nothing but a shirt and a modification of the *chiripa*, the native substitute for unmentionables. Bob Eckford, true to the memories of his native land, constructed for himself a wonderful garment of the nature of a kilt, out of a gaudily-striped *poncho*, which he called the '*gaucho* tartan.' I was the dandy of the party with my home-made clothes, which, however, had been borrowed so often by the others, that they soon began to present an appearance quite in harmony with the rest of our surroundings.

Such, then, was our life on the Pampas, so different from what most of us had been accustomed to—*so* different, that I remember being very much astonished to find by experience that nettles out there stung just as much as they do at home. And while on the subject of contrasts, I will end this chapter with a string of rather sentimental verses which were composed in some of our many spare hours. I won't say which of us had most right to be considered the author of this production, but we all had a hand in it. The reader must bear in mind the difference of our seasons, and also allow a little play for poetic exaggeration.

PORTRAITS OF THREE GENTLEMEN.—*The Pampas*, p. 200.

A SONG OF THE ANTIPODES.

'Have we then sought another world,
    Not yet to find content!
In grumbling here, as once at home,
    Full half our days are spent.

'When summer comes with Christmas flowers,
    And long December days,
Nought but the frosts and fogs of June
    Shall have our fickle praise.

'But cowering round the evening fire
    Of cold and dark July,
For January's genial breeze
    And undimmed suns we sigh.

'In autumn we desire to see
    October fresh and gay;
The thoughts of spring are fixed upon
    The withered leaves of May.

'Perspiring o'er our Christmas fare,
    In vain we long for snow;
Midsummer day, we fain would sit
    Beside the Yule log's glow.

'Oh, foolish man! who never is,
    But always *to be* blest!
How slow to learn the present's gifts
    Are for the present best!

'Happy the few whom fate hath taught
    To keep their hearts in tune
With sweet December's whispering breath,
    And with the storms of June!

'The bracing south, the balmy north,
    Alike rich gifts will send
To him who every wind of life
    Can welcome as a friend.'

CHAPTER XI.

THE INDIANS AGAIN!

TOWARDS the end of January, Jim left us; the fact was, that so long as the Indians continued to threaten our part of the country, Desmond and Eckford did not care to increase their stock, and there was not work for Jim about the place. Accordingly he went to a place on the other side of Villa Grande, a native *estancia*, where, if he was to be believed, they 'didn't give him grub enough to supper a decent rat on.' About the same time, an addition was made to our establishment in the shape of an old native woman, who was engaged to attend to the cooking—no very pleasant job in this hot weather. By night she slept under the *ramada;* by day she presided over our open-air kitchen, where her labours chiefly consisted in smoking cigarettes, and scolding and hitting Senecio, when she could catch him. She was the most ugly and wrinkled specimen of humanity I ever saw; and unfortunately her temper was no better than her looks. Senecio, for his part, was doubtless extremely 'aggravating,' and our cook's shrill voice could be constantly heard denouncing him, while he probably was grinning at a safe distance. The young rascal had picked up from Jim the English groom's trick of *hissing*, as if he was rubbing down a horse; and he took great delight in making this peculiar sound from morning to night, all the more that it seemed to drive Saturnina—that was her name—quite frantic, so that she was with difficulty restrained from throwing everything within reach, even to our dinner, at his thick, woolly head. He was told to stop it; but when none of us were by, he insisted on teasing the old woman, till at last his mischievousness got him into veritable hot water.

We had just sat down one evening after our work, and were shouting to Senecio to bring the tea, when for answer there came a loud scream, and a succession of yells that might have been heard half a mile off. Our first thought was of Indians, and seizing our revolvers, we rushed out to find Senecio writhing and yelling on the ground, and Saturnina standing at bay with the steaming pot in her hand, the contents of which she had just thrown over him. We hastened to pick up the boy, who kept screaming that he was murdered, and found that he had been severely scalded by the boiling water. Saturnina, her black eyes glistening with rage, vowed she would kill him, and looked as if she were sorry the pot was empty, and she could not serve us in the same way.

Luckily for poor Senecio, Desmond had been a medical student, and knew what was to be done; and luckily, too, he was not unprovided with proper medicament, in the shape of a bottle of chalk tooth-powder, which he made into a paste and plastered over Senecio's scalded skin, so that in a few days he was as lively and impudent as ever, though he declined to come within twenty yards of Saturnina, unless under the protection of one of us.

This was not the only time that Desmond's smattering of medical knowledge came in handy. The natives had a great opinion of his skill, and indeed he was very successful in curing two or three cases of sores, in the following way. He washed the place well with salt and water, and bound a piece of clean linen rag round it, giving strict directions that the patient was not to take this off till a certain day, when the wound, being kept clean, was almost sure to have healed. One case was not so easily dealt with. Our old cook had proclaimed herself as suffering from a complication of internal disorders, and pains which shifted about to every part of her body. Desmond declined prescribing for such a case; but she pestered us all, till at last Bob Eckford undertook to cure her, and set about it in a remarkable fashion. The old lady being directed to lie down on the ground, Dr. Eckford walked solemnly round her, reciting in a loud and serious tone—

> 'My name is Norval, on the Grampian hills
> My father feeds his flock, a frugal swain.'

A draught of Gregory's powder in gin-and-water was then prepared by me, acting as the doctor's assistant; and Eckford having muttered over it a few words of hocus-pocus that sounded like a somewhat vague reminiscence of the Latin grammar, made the patient drink it up without drawing breath, and pledged his reputation that on that day three weeks she would be completely restored to health. And I have no doubt that she would have declared the cure complete; but before the appointed date, Senecio's surgical case came about, and she had left us.

On the whole, one can do pretty well in camp without the aid of any physician, except Drs. Air and Exercise; and as for apothecaries' shops, our well and all the water about was strongly impregnated with sulphate of magnesia, familiarly known as Epsom Salts. But occasionally surgical aid is sadly wanted. Indeed, I had reason to know how one of the most thankworthy features of civilisation is—the dentist. I suffered a week of the most intense misery from toothache, unable to rest by day or to sleep by night. With this experience, I am inclined to think that the toothache is one of the most real and serious evils of life ; and not the least part of it is, that nobody sympathizes with you much. But if you laugh at me, I only wish you may be put in my place, and feel what it is to be tormented by a wretched, insignificant little grinder, without hope of cure or alleviation. I must say my companions, though I was quite a nuisance to them, were very kind, and Desmond went the length of several ineffectual attempts to extract the tooth with a bullet mould, to which, in my agony, I submitted with fortitude, nay, with a wild joy, feeling it some satisfaction to be thus revenged on the offending member. But Desmond's well-meant efforts only made things worse, and at last, unable to bear it longer, I had made up my mind to go to Rosario, between one and two hundred miles distant, to see a dentist, and was to have started next morning, when the toothache suddenly left me, and had the kindness not to come back again.

In spite of the pain, I could not help smiling at the remedy which one of our *peons* gravely suggested as a never-failing one. It was nothing else than this, to dip a small piece of the skin of a jaguar in melted mare's grease, and hold it to the tooth for a time, when in three days, he promised me, the said tooth, however large and firm, would loosen and drop out!

The natives are most ignorant and superstitious in medical matters. Their great remedy is mare's grease, applied externally, which is also used for lights, for softening hides, for oiling cart wheels; in fact, it is difficult to say what it is not used for, besides being the Holloway's Ointment of these parts. But they have other methods of cure, unknown to the faculty. Our *peons* used to make a cross of weeds in the *corral* to keep off infectious disorders from the animals. I have seen a native following a horse with a sore back into which the fly had got; at every hoof mark, the man lifted a clod, scratched a cross and replaced it, and at every mark so made he assured me that a maggot dropped out of the horse's back. Another horse being ill from eating a poisonous weed, one of the *peons* tried to cure it by breaking a new-laid egg in the middle of its forehead ; and when it died, he declared that the egg could not have been applied right in the middle, or the horse would surely have recovered.

To return to our violent cook : after her outbreak against Senecio, we thought she had better look out for another situation, and with our old world notions, gave her a week's notice to leave. But before the week was out, a fresh cause of quarrel had arisen on a score not unknown in the old world, that of 'followers.' A very rascally-looking native had been in the habit of paying visits to her, and seemed always to take it as a matter of course that he was to be our guest. But Desmond, not liking his looks, had warned him not to come back. He did come back one evening ; whereupon, in the absence of the masters of the station, I undertook to air my Spanish by ordering him to be off. In a minute Saturnina came furiously upbraiding me, and from her shrill harangue I gathered that the stranger was her husband, and that she was so shocked at this violation of the duties of hospitality that she would not remain another hour in our house. So, without delay, she ripped up her mattress, turned out the straw inside, stuffed into it the small bundle of articles which composed her wardrobe, treated Senecio to a final shake of her fist, and haranguing till she was out of hearing, trudged off to join her husband, who had removed a little way off, and was placidly smoking till his wife should be ready to accompany him.

Having once known the luxury of a hired cook, we could not return to the drudgery of the pot; and after a brief interval, in which Senecio was tried in this capacity, and found grievously wanting, we were lucky enough to fall in with a substitute, no other than the Italian organ-grinder with whom I had travelled in the train to Villa Grande. He had been as far as Cordova in the exercise of his profession, but had either been unsuccessful or imprudent, for he was now pennilessly and cheerfully grinding his way back over the camp, *whither* he scarcely seemed to know or care. He stopped at our station for a night, and as he appeared to be a smart fellow and willing to work, we persuaded him to stay to be our cook, and to make himself generally useful, like the rest of us. Besides, as Bob Eckford said, his instrument might serve for a defence against the Indians, and would certainly help to pass away our dull evenings.

So, to Senecio's great delight, Signor Baptista and his organ took up their abode with us, at the remuneration of fifteen dollars a month, with board and lodging; and every evening we regaled our ears with the music which drives crusty old gentlemen in

London to such despair. As for Senecio, this instrument proved to him a means of moral as well as artistic training; the promise of being allowed to take a turn at it produced quite a surprising amount of good behaviour in him. Bob Eckford, too, was at first enthusiastic about our new acquisition. He accompanied all the tunes on his concertina. I joined the orchestra with a jingling instrument of the nature of a triangle; and our concerts were so successful, that our neighbours used to ride over to spend the evening with us, as readily as boys seek the society of a companion who has had a cake sent him.

We were just like great schoolboys with our toy, of which, like schoolboys, we got tired before long. Unfortunately the organ only played six tunes, and though *Donna e mobile* and *A che la morte* are very pretty, one can easily hear too much of them. And if not the organ, at least its owner, soon got equally tired of us. It was not in his nature to remain in any one place for more than a month together, and he grew so restless that at last we had to let him go, with regret, for he was a good-natured fellow, and helped to keep us lively. So, one morning, he wrapped his wages in what seemed to have once been a handkerchief, put a lump of bread and a rib or two of cold mutton in his pocket, likewise a bottle of water, shouldered his instrument, and fared forth into the wilderness in as matter-of-course a fashion as if he had been merely deserting Bayswater to try his luck in St. John's Wood.

It will be seen that our life in camp was often rather dull, in spite of its healthiness and freedom. The fact is, that after having been brought up as we had been, few men can altogether relish the Robinson Crusoe form of existence till custom has made it a second nature, when again they may be found to have lost all taste for the privileges of a civilised community. The other day I met a friend who had been on an Argentine camp for twenty years, and had run home for a two months' look at the old country. But he declared that he didn't enjoy it. The bustle and the hurry troubled him; fashionable society made him yawn; he couldn't bear the continual brick walls and chimney-pots, and he vowed that the anxiety of catching a train took away ten years from his life.

I confess that, enthusiastic as I was on my arrival, I, as well as my companions, came to be not long of knowing what it was to have too much of such a good thing as this wild life is. We had perhaps promised ourselves, that one of the great pleasures of such a life would be the total absence of the books which we had hated so much at school;

but I can remember the delight of us all, when, soon after our organ-grinder left us, a box of books arrived, sent by some good friend in England. They were not the best of books; our correspondent had got them at a second-hand book shop, and his instructions were to prefer those in the smallest print, as taking up less room; but how glad we were to see them, even to an odd volume of last century sermons by some long-forgotten bishop, which we used for falling asleep over on Sundays. Among others, there were Knight's *Half-hours of English History; Selections from Browning* (a capital book for a small library—a little goes a long way); Drinkwater's *Siege of Gibraltar;* Pepys' *Diary* (which you could begin and leave off at any place, and forget the beginning by the time you had got to the end); two bound volumes of *Once a Week;* Carlyle's *Lectures on Hero-Worship;* Scott's *Tales of a Grandfather,* and three or four of his novels (we got tired of them, but not before they were dropping to pieces); Prescott's *History of Philip the Second;* a Treatise on Veterinary Surgery (very useful, though not amusing); Bruce's *Travels in Abyssinia;* Hood's *Comic Poems;* a cookery book; Dumas' *Three Musketeers;* and last, but certainly not least, Dickens' *American Notes,* and *David Copperfield.* The only time I was nearly quarrelling with good-natured

Bob Eckford was over *David Copperfield*. We all wanted to read it first.

So the days went by till the end of February, every one like another; and we began to wish that we could see a little—just a little—of the Indians, to vary the peaceable and somewhat tiresome monotony of looking after sheep, and carting out to the *estancia* materials for our fences. But all this time the Indians kept away, and we had no chance of executing our plan of uniting to punish them, if they attempted to make another raid.

One afternoon, Desmond and I had strolled out to see if we could not get a shot at a deer. We were about a mile from the house, when I caught sight of what looked like a large animal moving among the long grass, about a hundred and fifty yards off.

'What's that?' I exclaimed, calling Desmond's attention to it.

'I should say a lion,' he replied, after shading his eyes with his hand and taking a good long look at it.

Here was an exciting piece of sport! I had never had a fair chance of a shot at any real wild beast bigger than a *biscacho*—we didn't count ostriches—and hastily cocking my rifle, I advanced to stalk the animal, which for the moment was hidden among the grass. Presently I caught sight of it again; it was coming towards us. I raised my rifle, and was taking a steady aim, when suddenly Desmond knocked up the barrel, shouting—

'Hold hard! It's a man, I declare!'

My bullet whizzed harmlessly into the air, and no sooner had the report died away, than we could both distinguish a faint cry; and on running forward a few yards, saw that it was indeed a man whom I had so nearly shot at.

A man, but in such a state that he scarcely resembled a human being! A native, almost naked, with his skin blistered and torn, and scarcely the strength to murmur a few words in his own language, much less to raise himself from the ground. Good heavens! how thankful I was not to have fired on him, for a deliberate shot at that distance would have been too unlikely to miss its mark.

The poor fellow was so exhausted that we thought he would have died on the spot.

'*Agua, agua!*' he muttered, looking at us with such imploring eyes as I should hope never to see in my bitterest foe.

Without waiting to learn how he came into such a plight, I left Desmond to look after him, and ran as hard as I could to the house, heedless of the hot afternoon sun that made me drip with perspiration.

In about ten minutes I was back again on a barebacked horse, with water and spirits and biscuits. Eckford and Senecio followed hard at my heels, bringing food enough to feed a dozen starving people.

The unfortunate man drank greedily, and tried to eat, but his stomach seemed to refuse food. A little gin, however, did so much for him, that we thought we might get him up to the house. So sore and emaciated was he, that he could not sit on a horse; we lifted him up and carried him between us, not without fears that he might die in our arms at any step of the way.

Arrived safely at the house, we put him to bed, and did all we could to make him comfortable, giving him small quantities of nourishment at a time, and applying mare's grease to his skin, which almost all over his body was in such a state that he could scarcely bear it touched. Before the evening was over, he confirmed our suspicions that this was the work of the Indians; and next morning, feeling much better, he told us the whole story.

He was a deserter from the army—that he frankly confessed, glancing wistfully at us, as if to ask if we would give him up. He had deserted on account of a severe punishment inflicted on him, as he said, only by the spite of his officer; and having heard that some of his countrymen who were in trouble had joined the Indians and been well treated by them, he made his way south, and before long fell in with a band which seemed to be hanging about the outskirts of the settlements. They had made him prisoner, tied him to a horse, and carried him towards their own country; but after one day's journey, they next morning stripped him of everything but his drawers, and with fiendish cruelty turned him loose to perish beneath the sweltering sun. But, determined not to die without an effort, he tore up the rag of clothing left to him, so as to make some sort of covering for his back; and then, crawling on his hands and knees, and availing himself of such shade as the grass could give, he had painfully returned northwards, finding scarcely anything to eat except grasshoppers, and for the last two days being in the greatest distress for want of water. He had given up hope and lain down to die, when he heard a gun not far off, and rousing himself for a last effort came towards us, too weak to cry out or to rise to his feet.

This tale revived in our minds all the horror which we had been accustomed to associate with the name of these too near neighbours of ours, of whose cruelty we had this new proof before us, and a warning of what might be our own fate, if courage or caution failed us. We kept their victim for a few days. As soon as he had picked up some strength he seemed anxious to be off, naturally enough, considering how near we were to the post at Villa Grande; so we let him go his ways, and heard no more about him. But you may be sure that for some time we kept a good look-out. One or two evenings we saw lights glimmering about at some distance from our house, and took them for signals made by a party of Indians who were reconnoitring us. We accordingly fired a shot or two to show that we were on the alert, and sat up all night to watch; but nothing happened, and probably we had been deceived by will-o'-the-wisps, or lights of a similar kind, which are to be seen out there when the camps are as dry as a bone, and are looked on by the natives with much superstitious awe.

But from other quarters we heard reports of the Indians having been seen hovering about, and were kept in such a state of uneasiness that I believe we all heartily wished they would come and let us have it out with them. We had plenty of firearms, and so long as we were not taken by surprise, had no doubt of being able to defend ourselves, this time, against any number of these savages, who are such utter cowards so long as they have not their enemy at a great disadvantage, and will not face one-twentieth of their number of Europeans in the open field. Then, if we could only contrive to communicate with any of our neighbours, such arrangements had been agreed upon among the owners of stations round about, that in a few hours an ample force might be expected to arrive at any point of danger. 'The Camp Insurance Association,' as Bob Eckford dubbed this militia, could muster some thirty men, and as our commander we had appointed Darrell, the oldest and most experienced of the English settlers, whose station lay in the centre of the district exposed to these attacks. We made no doubt but that, if we could once have a brush at the enemy, we should be rid of them for a long time to come; and some of us, especially young fellows like me, who didn't know what fighting was, grew quite eager to have a chance of displaying our valour.

At last it came. One morning about an hour after daybreak, just as we were about to drive out the sheep, young Clark came galloping over, his horse all in a lather, to tell us that a large band of Indians had paid them a visit the night before. Luckily they were not taken unawares; having been warned in good time of the enemy's approach, they hastily killed a sheep, brought it and a good supply of water inside of the house, and prepared to defend themselves, taking up their position on the flat, parapetted roof. The Indians surrounded them, at first silently, then with a storm of hideous yells; but they fled in confusion when a hand grenade was flung into the thick of the crowd and exploded among their feet, killing and terrifying men and horses. They remained in the neighbourhood all night, and must have removed their dead and wounded; for though the grass was stained with blood all round the spot where the grenade had burst, no bodies were to be found. Very early in the morning they went away, driving off all the horses and cattle they could find, and taking their course, not as usual southwards, but towards the west, as if bent on further mischief. Clark had ridden over to us without delay, and his partner was giving the alarm at two stations to the north-east of us. If by mid-day a dozen or so of men could be got together at the Simpsons' old station, lying to our south-west, a dash might be made at the marauders before they could retreat.

In ten minutes our two *peons* were in the saddle, galloping north and west with the fiery cross, that is to say, leaves torn out of a book of cigarette papers, on which were hurriedly scribbled the news of the Indians being near, and the name of the rendezvous.

We knew we might rely on our neighbours at the different stations; and without waiting for his breakfast, Desmond rode off himself to Villa Grande, if possible to stir up the Commandante to action. The rest of us breakfasted and waited an hour or two, in case we should see something of the Indians. Then leaving Senecio, who was frightened into sobriety, in charge of sheep, house, and in fact the whole station, till the *peons* should come back, we set off, duly armed and equipped, for the place of meeting.

CHAPTER XII.

THE CHASE.

WE arrived at the rendezvous about noon, but three men were there before us, and as we approached we saw Darrell riding up from the opposite direction, upon a big piebald camel of a beast with ears that would have done credit to a mule, and paces that nobody could put up with except its master, who found them so smooth that in affectionate moments he used to call this monster his old arm-chair. All of these men were our nearest neighbours, and had known the Simpsons; and when we looked at the black ruins, and the weed-grown garden and *corrals*, and thought of the cruel murder of our poor friends, we wanted nothing more to excite us against the Indians, thinking every minute wasted that was delayed in the pursuit.

Soon afterwards Desmond arrived from Villa

Grande. He had seen the Commandante, who had sworn, pulled his moustache, and vowed that in an hour he would be after the marauders, with every man he could get together. But Desmond waited for more than an hour and saw no signs of this force, except a broken drum which was being beaten up and down the town to give the alarm, and which certainly seemed to do so, in one sense; so he came on, hoping that the natives would follow him not too late. He was followed by a message from the Commandante, again assuring him that by one o'clock he might be expected with sixty men ('Why didn't he say six hundred while he was at it?' growled Bob Eckford); but one o'clock came, and the degenerate Spanish cavalry did not appear. We afterwards heard that they did turn up some thirty strong, about sunset, and finding that we had not waited for them, fell back and took up a strategic position 'to protect the town'—slanderous people went the length of saying that they all ran away on seeing a flock of ostriches in the distance; but the Commandante afterwards bragged so loudly of what he *would* have done, if he had come across the enemy, that this story surely can't be true.

But all this while, our friends had kept dropping in singly or in little knots; and as the day wore on, we began to get impatient to be off. About two o'clock, a clever little native, who had been sent out to reconnoitre, came back with the report that he had discovered the trail of the Indians, who seemed to have been making for the Simpsons' place, and then suddenly to have struck off south on discovering that it had been already plundered; so they were probably not the same band which had been there before. At this news we could no longer be held in. We were quite enough to deal with any number of Indians, so we said, and our native allies were not worth waiting for—indeed, they were more likely to be in the way than otherwise. Darrell, whom we had agreed to obey as captain, had hitherto checked our eagerness; but now he, as well as all the most sensible men of the party, agreed that we could wait no longer if we were to make sure of overtaking the enemy, and the word was given to be off.

By this time there were sixteen of us Europeans, mostly Englishmen and Germans; two more overtook us before the evening, and we were accompanied by about half a dozen natives, all servants except one *vaqueano*, who had ridden out from Villa Grande as a volunteer, and, I must confess, did much to redeem the character of his countrymen by the coolness and smartness which he showed.

His name was Rufino, or *El Ñato*, 'the flat-nosed,' as he was more commonly called by his countrymen. It was he who first found the Indians' trail, and he was most useful as a guide throughout the march.

This was the first and last time in my life that I ever took part in anything of the sort, and I was too much excited, perhaps, to be a very accurate observer, yet one could not but be struck by the appearance of this motley militia, made up of men of all nations, in all varieties of free-and-easy costume. Each man had a led horse with him, and his rifle and a revolver; then of course we all carried a small bag or other parcel of provisions, and at every saddle hung a demijohn or cow-horn flask of water, or, for want of anything better, a bottle slung in a stocking. It reminded me of nothing so much as of a meet in England; only that when one goes to hunt men on the Pampas, one is not so particular about one's hat and boots, as when one goes to hunt foxes in Leicestershire. And, oddly enough, we hadn't ridden along much more than five minutes before a big grey fox actually did break from under the feet of the foremost horses, and went scudding over the plain, leaving behind it a scent that needed no hound's nose to follow.

'Tallyho!' shouted one young fellow, rising in his

stirrups and waving on the rest; and then, with shouts and laughter, about half-a-dozen men galloped off hard at the heels of the frightened animal, and the singular spectacle was afforded of a real fox-hunt on the Pampas. Our foreign friends thought they had gone mad, and some of the older men yelled out to the thoughtless fellows to come back; indeed, Darrell used language on the occasion which would not have disgraced a zealous master of hounds; and when these too sportive members of his pack had pulled up and come back, he used his authority as captain to fine them a bottle of beer all round for leaving the main body without orders, and scolded them soundly for not sparing their horses; and, indeed, before we got to the end of the march, we needed every bit of their strength.

'This business may turn out to be not so much of a joke as you think,' he said; but of course there were some who smiled at such a notion, as if they knew better.

A little more than a league brought us on the track of the Indians, a broad swathe of broken-down grass and freshly trampled ground, that could not lead us astray. Our native guide declared from the traces that it must be several hours since they passed; but, encumbered as they were with the

Clarkes' animals, we made no doubt of coming up with them, and pushed on eagerly at a good canter, two or three scouts always galloping some way in front, and straining their eyes for a glimpse of the retreating band. It was probable that they were in a hurry, for at one place where the ashes of their fires told us that they had halted, we came upon several carcases, not half eaten or cut up, of bullocks which had no doubt been killed lest their slower pace should impede the flight. Not far off there were also two mounds of freshly-turned earth, which we supposed to be Indian graves. At the sight of these young Clarke smiled and patted his revolver, as if to say this was part of his work. Not the least evil of having to do with these cruel savages is, that one is apt to forget they are fellow-creatures, and so rejoice in their death as if they were wild beasts. I can't say I ever got quite as far as this, but I was long enough in the colony to understand the feelings of men who are always exposed to their depredations.

'When you have to choose between killing and being killed,' said Desmond, 'you come to feel less squeamish, and think as little about it as a stockjobber does about cheating.'

'It's a clear flying in the face of Providence not to clear them off,' said our old friend the American

Major. 'Tigers ain't a circumstance to these critturs for cruelty and beastliness.'

'It's got to be done, so there's no use talking about it.' That was the way Darrell summed up the matter.

It was supposed that this band of marauders consisted not only of Indians, but to some extent of natives who had joined them and adopted their way of life, escaped criminals, deserters from the army, and other bad characters. Such renegades could expect no mercy, as it was understood they would show none; and though they might fight desperately when turned to bay, none of us for a moment fancied that in a fair field they could possibly get the best of us.

On we went, and the most lively of us soon lost all desire for unnecessary exertion. The day was as hot as usual at this time of year, and the cloud of dust caused by such a large party riding together helped to make our mouths so dry that most of us had exhausted our supplies of water before we had been much more than an hour on the way. Indeed, every draught only seemed to make us long for more. I fear that the potations of *caña* in which we had tried to beguile our impatience while waiting at the hut, must have had something to do with it; at least we noticed that the natives, who steadily refused to touch spirits or to smoke, seemed to suffer much less from thirst. In spite of this, some men went on smoking cigarettes and sipping *caña* so long as they had any, and the result was that they were driven almost frantic. We had to send one back in the care of his *peon;* the poor fellow, after behaving like a madman, fell off his horse in a fit, and seemed as if knocked down by a sunstroke or a fit of apoplexy. I was rather astonished to see that one of the party, whom I shall not name, a man whom I had always looked upon as the most selfish, ill-conditioned curmudgeon I knew, yet offered the last drop out of his flask to wet the other's lips with. Heaven knows it was no small bit of Christian charity, this, and I thought I would not be so hasty to determine on people's characters for the future.

'I think I'd sell my birthright, if I had one, for a bottle of gingerbeer,' whispered Eckford to me; and I could sympathize with him.

Here was a danger we had not counted on, and one far more to be dreaded than any number of the cowardly robbers we were pursuing. We now got upon a large tract of burned grass, where the black dust rose thicker and hotter, and increased our sufferings. To halt or return were equally out of the question. We were already more than half-way to a spot where our *vaqueano*, who knew the country well, assured us that there was an old well, and all we could do was to hurry on to it, with the dreadful suspicion that it might be dried up, or that this man might be wrong. We were too little accustomed to trust in a native's sagacity or truthfulness.

Now that it is all over, I can feel some satisfaction in recalling this unusual experience of life; but at the time it was wholly painful in the extreme. I felt as if I could have given anything for a good draught of ditch water; I almost hated a man beside me who was draining a few last drops from the bottom of his flask. I thought of thirsty travellers in the great desert of Sahara, of shipwrecked sailors drifting about on a raft, of the prisoners in the Black Hole, and wondered how human nature could endure the pain of thirst for many hours. It is impossible at this distance of time to describe my sensations fully; when I think of it now, it seems like a burning dream. I only remember that first there came a thick muddy feeling in my mouth, then it grew dry and smarting, and my tongue seemed swollen so that I could scarcely speak, my lips felt hard and crisp; and I should say few of the party suffered less than I did. We did not try to talk, but rode steadily on, doing what we could to relieve ourselves by sucking bullets, or, what was safer and more effectual, the necks of bottles,—I found an iron nail of use. But after a time we lost even the power of suction, and men took to wetting their lips with the perspiration from their shirts. Fancy a thirty-mile ride under a blazing sun in such a plight, you luxurious young gentlemen who can't travel by express train without getting out at every station to have a glass of '*bittaw*'!

Our horses behaved admirably. All covered with dust, their nostrils almost closed up by it, their sufferings must have been very great; but they galloped bravely on, as if knowing that their only chance of relief lay in our intelligence. But their instinct was first to tell us that relief was near at hand. When the sun was sinking low, though the cooler air seemed to give us no alleviation of our burning thirst, suddenly our poor beasts threw up their heads, and began whinnying and straining forwards in a wild state of excitement; they smelt the water half a mile off, and at the same time Rufino, our *vaqueano*, who was riding on in front, appeared waving his hat, and giving us to understand that the well was not far off.

Then our parched tongues loosened, we found our voices to give a hoarse shout of joy, and away raced the whole cavalcade towards the spot where we could already see the edging of high green grass that marked the position of the well.

Neither the man nor the horses were mistaken. It was a well; quite a large pond, about eight feet below the level of the ground, with a slope down to the brink of the water on one side, by which the animals might approach to drink; and it was in a state that I can only call a delirium of joy, that we spurred our willing horses up to it. Then in a minute the whole body were struggling to reach the water, the foremost slipping and trampling in its muddy brink.

Bitter disappointment! Water there was in plenty, but water foul and fetid, which for months had been stagnating in that deserted spot. A green scum covered all its surface, only removed to show the mud thrown up by our horses' hoofs; the bones of a dead animal lay half covered at one side; from the other, three or four snakes slipped off into the grass. This was the well which we had strained to reach, picturing it in our fancies, perhaps, as a gushing, limpid stream, every drop more pure and precious than diamonds; now the smell and the sight were enough to make us pause, mad with thirst as we were.

At any other time we should have drawn back with disgust, but it was now a question of life or death. Our horses were already drinking greedily of the foul pool; all we could do was to strain it through a canvas saddle-bag, and gulp it down hastily. Even that draught was welcome, but we needed no warning to drink as little as we could. Three or four men turned sick and faint on the spot, and two were so bad, that if it had not been simply impossible to leave them, they would have gone no farther. I noticed that these, as well as the man who had been knocked up early in the afternoon, were all big, strong-looking Englishmen, proud of their beef and beer constitutions. Two wiry Italians who were with us, and at whose frugal ways of living we had often sneered, had certainly the laugh on their side that day, for they bore both fatigue and thirst better than any of us. They would not drink the water of the pond, but washed their heads and wetted their shirts in it, so that the moisture might enter through the pores.

We stopped here for about two hours. Before supper we held a council to determine what should be done. The almost unanimous opinion was to go on. The trail of the Indians was always before us, leading straight forward in the direction of a deserted fort on the old frontier line, where the natives assured us we should find a plentiful supply of excellent water. Riding by night, we might hope to suffer less from thirst, and it was probable that we should overtake the enemy before another day was over. After going through so much, it seemed out of the question to turn back without firing a shot. So it was decided.

'And we'll make a well of Indian blood,' muttered somebody, expressing the fierce determination of the rest.

Between nine and ten o'clock we started again. All the 'spunk' had been taken out of us by this time, and we rode carefully at a jog-trot, trying not to distress our horses, as well as to reserve our own energy for the attack, which we promised ourselves should at last reward us for all that we were undergoing.

We had a good moon most of the way, and the night was cooler and more pleasant. Our sufferings from thirst were by no means at an end, but they were not so bad that we could not console ourselves by thinking of the well which we should reach early in the morning. Then, to our great joy, the dew began to fall, and we were able to dismount and suck the wet blades of half-withered grass. This way of quenching our thirst caused some delay, but we did not care to press on, as it would be better not to come up with the Indians by night, and it was supposed that now they could not be far ahead of us. So we rode on doggedly in silence, and kept a good look-out, seeing nothing, however, but the broad road of trampled grass in front of us, and hearing nothing but the melancholy hooting of the owls on either side of the path, or occasionally the strange noise made by the *biscachos* underground,—a noise composed of a cough, a sneeze, a grunt, and a bray all mixed into one extraordinary sound, which might well have terrified any one not so familiar with it as all of us were. Desmond used to declare that nothing came so near to it, as when I attempted to sing 'In the Bay of Biscay, O!'

When at last day began to break, we found that we had come into a more undulating and diversified country. Several shrubs which we were not accustomed to see met our eyes, and on little ridges in the distance were patches of *monte* or wood. Surely water could not be far off?

We were in almost as great need of rest, having ridden, as we calculated, not less than twenty-five leagues ; and it was with no small satisfaction that, just as the rim of the sun peeped out, we caught sight of the fort for which we were making, on the top of a slight elevation not a league off. I was rather surprised at the appearance of it. I had expected to see one or two ruined huts, but it turned out to be a building of some size, and, on drawing nearer, we found that it had once been a regular fortification.

Our horses now showed the same eagerness as on coming to the well the night before; and tired as we all were, we galloped up the hill and dashed through the single narrow gap which served as entrance to the fortification, with so little caution, that if we had had to do with a bold and skilful enemy, and he had chosen to lie in ambuscade there, it would most likely have gone hard with us.

But not a soul did we see within the walls. Only, as we poured in, the deer and ostriches bounded out in flocks from the rank weeds which filled every empty space, and fled, pursued by a few shots, one or two of which took effect. For one minute the deserted enclosure was the scene of a strange awakening of life, as when one removes the stone that covers a nest of ants; then all was abandoned to us. But we cared little to look about us, except for water; and water we did not fail to find,—two wells of it,—honest, drinkable water,—such, indeed, as a London ratepayer might turn up his nose at, but such as seemed to us more delicious than the richest vintages, or the most artfully compounded beverages. I think I must have drunk a gallon. I never enjoyed anything so much. My feeling and that of others was, that we longed to be able to throw ourselves bodily into it.

Here we now disposed ourselves to breakfast and

take our ease for a little, intending to resume the pursuit as soon as horses and men should be sufficiently refreshed, after a journey rather longer than the distance from London to Salisbury. A fire was lit; a deer, whose leg had been broken by a shot, was secured, killed, and put on the spit; and before we sat down to eat, we took good care that our horses had a feast of the *alfalfa*, a kind of long grass which grew abundantly throughout the enclosure. It was worth all we had gone through to sit down comfortably to a good meal, which we had so well deserved; and in spite of our fatigue, most of us were now in excellent spirits.

'This is every bit as exciting as anything I ever read in a book,' said Desmond at breakfast; and I only wish that Fenimore Cooper or Mayne Reid had been there to give a worthy description of all the incidents of our expedition.

After breakfast a council of war was held, but I, and two or three more of the younger fellows, thinking that our advice would not be wanted, chose to spend this time in looking round us.

The place in which we had now taken up our quarters was, as I said, one of the forts of the old frontier line, which had evidently been designed as a post of considerable strength. It occupied an enclosure of about five acres, surrounded by a low *adóba* wall and a dry ditch. Within this was a large square building, also of dry earth, and a few huts. The spaces between were almost entirely filled with patches of *alfalfa* grass, and rank weeds rising to the height of six or seven feet, among which, however, we found some peaches and watermelons growing no less luxuriantly in a part that had once been cultivated as a garden. The square building, or citadel, as it might be called, had walls of considerable height and thickness, loopholed all round, and at each corner of the flat roof was a tower with crumbling parapets, where a cannon had probably been mounted, and from which we had a wide look-out over the surrounding country.

The scene that met our eyes was more like a 'view' than anything that we were accustomed to, and might have even been called beautiful. In the direction we had come from, indeed, nothing was to be seen but leagues of flat, dry grass, a dull waste which Mr. Browning must have seen very much transfused by the warm light of imagination, or of spring, when he wrote—

> 'Fancy the Pampas' sheen,
> Miles of gold and green,
> Where the sunflowers blow
> In a solid glow.'

But before us, towards the Indian country, the

ground was more rough, even rugged, diversified with little copses, gigantic thistles, and other plants seldom seen in our neighbourhood; and at the foot of the rising ground on which the fort stood was a wide *laguna*, several miles long, prettily fringed with cactus and *chanar* plants, and looking deliciously cool and clear in the morning sunshine. Just beneath the walls of the fort was a little cemetery, containing a roofless chapel, before which a rusty bell still hung, and four or five graves, each marked with a clumsy wooden cross. On coming nearer, we found that these graves had been dug so long ago that they could scarcely be distinguished among the coarse grass; and beside them lay the unburied skeleton of a man, still wearing his boots and rotting fragments of his clothing. If it had not been for this grim memento of the real world, we might have thought we had found our way into the enchanted palace of the Sleeping Beauty. A strange silence reigned through the deserted settlement, broken only, as we stood still and listened, by the tapping of some little beasts about the size of rats, which make a curious sound like a carpenter hammering nails into a coffin,—so, at least, it struck my imagination in such a scene. I forget what they used to be called.

There being no signs of the presence of the

Indians near the fort, it was decided to rest there all day, and to resume the pursuit in the evening. A halt, indeed, was absolutely necessary, not so much for our own sake as for that of our horses, which, already too lean after the drought of summer, were so fatigued that some of them did not seem to care for their food.

Four sentinels were placed on the towers, to be relieved every hour, and the orders were that the rest of us should not go far from the fort. So we dispersed to recreate ourselves in different ways. Some snatched a few winks of sleep; some strolled about, examining the ruins of the fort, and the unfamiliar plants that grew around it; others, of whom I was one, went off for a bathe. Eckford and I, and a small Italian that I had made friends with, having drawn lots to have the next turn on guard, lost no time in making for the banks of the *laguna*, and there, with some difficulty finding a spot where we could get at the edge without passing through a prickly hedge, stripped and plunged in to enjoy the long unknown luxury of a free swim in deep clear water.

I suppose about a dozen of us must have been a quarter of an hour disporting ourselves, ducking, splashing, chasing, and racing one another with shouts of glee, like so many schoolboys, and I, having swam out some two hundred yards, was lying on my back lazily paddling along, looking up to the cloudless sky above, and thinking how much pleasanter this was than to be lying in bed on a damp windy morning at home, when suddenly I got a start on hearing the sound of the chapel bell rung in quick sharp strokes as if to give the alarm, and turning on my breast saw a great commotion among all the other bathers, and the sentinels on the towers of the fort waving their hands and calling us back in haste. Everybody began to make for the shore, and I did not fail to strike out after the rest, shouting to my Italian friend, who was nearest me—

'What's the matter?'

'*Los Indios!*' he spluttered out in reply, with his mouth full of water; and the cry being taken up, a panic spread among the whole party, and we struggled desperately to get on land, fancying that we were in danger of being caught by the Indians, naked and defenceless.

'Where are they? where are they?' was each man's exclamation. Nobody could tell, but the bell continued to jangle in our ears, and the watchers on the towers seemed to beckon us to make haste; so we lost not a minute in scrambling out, covering ourselves with the mud of the clayey bank; then, scarcely waiting to huddle on a single garment, and snatching up the rest in our hands, we ran barefoot up the hill as if we were running for our lives.

We were relieved, and at the same time not very well pleased, on being received with a hearty laugh by some of our comrades, who from the walls had seen our alarm, and guessed the mistake we had made. But we were really wanted. The smoke of some camp-fires had just been seen about a league and a half from the fort, and it was supposed that this marked the spot where the Indians were halting in some *cañada*, or hollow.

'They may be off directly,' said Darrell. 'So get on your freshest horses, and let's make a dash at them and finish it.'

At the news of the enemy being so near, we forgot all our fatigue, and lost not a moment in preparing to set out. A few minutes of confusion, finishing our toilet, saddling our horses, looking to the loading of our weapons, and all was ready. Leaving two or three *peons* to take care of the rest of the horses, we trotted out of the fort, and soon hitting on the Indian trail which came within half a league of it, we rode briskly for the spot where the smoke could be clearly seen against the horizon. By the by, we were rather at a loss to know why these copper gentry had passed so near the fort without paying it a visit; one of the natives told us that they were afraid of the white men's graves in the cemetery; but whether this was so or not, I can't say.

Less than half an hour's smart riding brought us close to the smoke. We had walked up a slight rising ground to breathe our horses, and on reaching the top came suddenly in sight of the Indians, who, about a hundred strong, with more than twice that number of horses, were encamped in the middle of a depression of the ground, deep enough to be called a valley, if the slopes had not been so gradual. They could not have been much more than half a mile from us, but they were already preparing for a move; and the moment they saw us, they leaped on horseback, rounded up the rest of the animals, and in an incredibly short time were flying up the opposite slope with loud yells, their *ponchos* and lance plumes flying in the air.

Away we went, settling ourselves in our saddles, and urging our horses to their utmost speed. For two minutes there was the wild excitement of a charge. Darrell, who had hitherto been so cool and prudent, now fairly lost his head. Riding in front on his tall piebald, he shook his fist at the flying Indians, and roared at the pitch of his voice, '*Que vengan cobardes! Que vengan demonios?*' 'I was enticing them to come on,' he afterwards explained to us.

Then the whole band raised a shout, each man in his own tongue, which at such a moment came most familiar to him. '*Auf!*' bellowed a German beside me; '*Avanti!*' piped our Italians; '*Vamos!*' cried the natives; and the rest of us joined to give a genuine British cheer, as we swept down the grassy slope and dashed through the smouldering fires of the camp.

Our poor horses did their utmost, but it was too plain that, tired as they were, the Indians had the best of it from the first. One or two of our animals fell exhausted before we reached the other side of the valley, and a man at my side—I think it was young Clarke—rolled out of his saddle at the very beginning of the charge. He had fainted from fatigue. But the others spurred on, furious to think that the Indians should escape us after all. Finding that they gained ground, some of our men pulled up and brought their rifles into play, and for the first time perhaps this lonely spot heard the sharp reports and the whirr of bullets. But fired at such a range the shots fell low, and buried themselves in the ground, or *ricochetted* among the legs of the enemies' horses, two of which fell; the riders, however, were not a moment in leaping on to their spare horses and following the rest. Just as they reached the crest of the ridge, we saw one man throw up his arms and fall backward. Another jumped off like a cat, stripped the fallen man of some article of clothing, and then, clinging to his horse's neck, disappeared on the other side with the last of the band.

We tore up the slope, the last part of which was so steep as to try our horses severely and check the most eager of us; while the Indians, having had the advantage of the level ground, were far ahead when next we caught sight of them, and the rifle bullets we sent after them only struck up little harmless clouds of dust several hundred yards in their rear. There was nothing for it but to abandon the pursuit, and the first half-dozen riders drew up beside the body of the dead man.

He was lying on his back almost naked, with open mouth and eyes, and a thin stream of blood running down his side from a wound near the heart. We might have looked on the poor wretch's dusky, grimy skin, his thin body, his coarse black hair, his narrow repulsive features, with no more emotion than on a slain wild beast. But over him stood a dog, a gaunt, unkempt, mangy-looking mongrel, that was gazing into its master's hard-set face with speechless pity, and licking his senseless form, and

THE DEAD MAN'S FRIEND.—*The Pampas*, p. 244.

as we rode up, lifted its head and whined as if entreating us to call him back to life; and then, as doubting our good-will, placed its paws on the dead man and growled at us angrily, and at last laid its head in the pool of blood that was thickening by his side, and raised a long mournful howl. I believe the poor brute's sorrow touched the roughest of us, coming as a rebuke of 'man's inhumanity to man.' When we saw how this dumb animal could mourn over our fellow-creature slain by our hands, the curses that were being hurled after his companions seemed somehow to stick in our throats. Perhaps there are some bishops who have never preached such a good sermon as that half-starved cur did.

Out of respect for the poor brute's affection, we threw some earth over his master's body, and even then could hardly manage to drag it away with us. Eckford put a lasso round its neck, and declared he would adopt it. We then proceeded to put out of pain the two Indian horses lying wounded on the field, as also one of our own animals, which, through setting its foot in a hole, had broken its leg. Its rider in his fall had sprained his thumb, and this was all our loss in this celebrated engagement.

And now we were again called upon to admire the coolness and smartness of our *vaqueano*, who had done the most business-like piece of work of any of the party. Leaving us to do whatever shooting and shouting might seem desirable, he and another native had carefully considered the situation, and making a bend to the left had cut off a 'point' of the enemy's horses, which they had not been sharp enough in getting away, and which the Indians who were driving them at once deserted on finding themselves pursued, and likely to be separated from the main body. These were nearly all the animals they had taken from Clarkes', so that we recovered the spoil, if we were not so successful as David was in smiting the Amalekites. So well had Rufino behaved throughout this expedition, that we voted him worthy of receiving the freedom of any country but his own, and on our return subscribed to present him with a handsome testimonial of our esteem, in the shape of dollars, which, I regret to say, he wasted in gambling at Rosario. Afterwards he came to Darrell's place as *puestero*, and, I am told, has prospered in the world since then, and become keeper of a coffeehouse at Cordova.

On the ground where the Indians had encamped we found a few articles which they had left behind them in their hurry — two or three lances and *boleadores*, a very old and exceedingly dirty sheepskin jacket, a guanaco-skin saddle cover, and a whip made out of a cow-tail, which last I took for my share of the booty, and have it to this day.

With these trophies we returned leisurely to the fort, and laid ourselves out to enjoy the rest of the day after our morning's work. Bob Eckford and I went down to the lake, intending to have another bathe and lie lazily there all the afternoon. But before we had finished our first pipe, Bob would have it that he saw a large fish darting about in the smooth water, and grew so excited by reminiscences of his native Tweed, that he must needs try his luck with the rod, which was neither more nor less than an Indian lance, the tackle being supplied by twine and a bent pin, on which he put a fly artfully made up of the wings of a real fly and a little of his own red hair. I never had much zeal for angling, even in the most favourable circumstances; so, leaving him industriously whipping the water, without catching even the sight of a fin, I took a walk through the wood which fringed the *laguna*, and got into trouble. For, falling in with a prickly pear tree, I rashly proceeded to deal with the ripe yellow fruit, and soon found my fingers and my mouth smarting with innumerable little thorns, which I only got rid of after some days, and by the aid of a pair of tweezers. Here was another lesson that the little enemies of life are more troublesome than its serious dangers, for I fairly lost my temper over this annoyance, whereas the perils and hardships of our expedition had, after all, come wonderfully natural to me. As for wild beasts, I had ceased to have any fear of them, and though I was walking alone, did not in the least trouble myself about the risk of meeting a so-called 'lion' or 'tiger.' But the prickly pears went far towards spoiling my afternoon.

When I came back to Eckford, I found that he had not been able to get a single bite. Nor were some of our comrades much more successful who had been out shooting. Our presence seemed to have frightened away all the animals of the neighbourhood, and the bag of the whole party amounted to no more than two wild ducks and three or four small parrots. These were nothing among a score of hungry men, and we had to look about for some more substantial fare. Near the Indians' line of march we found a mare and colt which had been savagely goaded, and then abandoned as unable to keep up with the rest. The mother was already dead, and the *carranchas* had been at her carcase; the colt had two or three lance-wounds, and was not likely to be fit for anything; so it was killed, and cut into two pieces, which were roasted at separate fires. We found the *potro* meat uncommonly good eating; our game made a second course, and we had plenty of fruit for dessert, so that we dined quite sumptuously.

About these fires there is something to be said. All the wood near was of the cactus kind, too green to burn well, also not very easy to get at or to hew down with our knives; and as the dinner hour approached, the cooks found themselves rather hard put to it for a fire. So an unsentimental German, who was superintending the culinary operations, made use of two or three of the crosses on the graves in the cemetery, which, as he argued, were of no use to the dead men, but very convenient for us. Such a utilitarian way of looking at the matter shocked the natives dreadfully, and they warned us that some evil would certainly result from this act of sacrilege. Some of our party, too, thought it was a pity; but, after all, it made very little difference to the poor fellows who were dead and gone; and, on the other hand, we imitated the piety of the ancients by scraping up a fresh grave, and decently covering the skeleton which had lain there beneath so many storms and suns.

After dinner we were all too tired for anything else than sleep, so to bed we went in the open air, or within the buildings of the fort, as each man liked, and slept with double soundness for this night and the one before. But in the middle of the night, or rather, I think, it was towards morning, we were awakened by a great noise of neighing and trampling mingled with the shrill yells of a *peon*, and were aware of the galloping of many horses round our quarters. Up we sprang, shouting to each other and seizing our arms, for our first impression was that the Indians were upon us. But on running outside, all we saw by the moonlight was the last of our horses disappearing out of the enclosure in which we had left them peaceably asleep. It was a regular stampede.

Here was a pretty to-do! In a minute or two the whole party had turned out, and the fort became a Tower of Babel, everybody asking what had happened, how it had happened, and what was to be done? The natives earnestly assured us that we could have expected nothing else, and that no doubt the spirits of the men whose grave we violated had come to avenge themselves by frightening our horses. Some of us, of a more practical turn of mind, suggested that a lion had got among them. One thing certain was that they were gone, and this was no joke when we were a hundred miles from home.

We were, however, relieved to find that Darrell had kept three or four horses tied up to be ready for any sudden emergency. These were all safe, and with their aid we made no doubt of being able to recover our fugitive steeds. So, in the meantime, we went back to bed and took our fill of sleep, and in the morning two or three men rode out and found the horses grazing quietly less than a league off.

Most of us set off homewards at once, leaving a few who remained at the fort for a day or two. On our way back we met with no adventure, except seeing a mirage which deceived even the old stagers into thinking it a lake. What a cruel mockery this would have proved if we had fallen in with it two days before, when suffering so much from thirst!

Thus ended our great expedition into the south country; and though we had not been successful in coming fairly to blows with the Indians, our pursuit of them seemed to have had a good effect, for it was long before they appeared again in our neighbourhood. Our volunteer corps, however, was not disbanded, but, on the contrary, was more regularly organized, and made up to a strength of twenty-five efficient men, who used to meet once a week for drill at Villa Grande,—an opportunity of uniting business with pleasure which was sufficiently appreciated to make the attendance pretty regular. A uniform, too, was adopted,—serge blouses, white trousers, and long boots, in which I venture to say that the corps with whom I first had the honour to smell a very little powder, looked more smart and soldier-like than any other military body in the country.

I ought to mention that the dead Indian's dog was brought home by Bob Eckford, who loved all animals, however ugly. This was the ugliest of beasts,—rusty black in colour, with patches of grey, tall and thin, with a long bushy tail, a blunt nose, and little peering eyes. It had none of the frankness and good-nature which we are accustomed to expect from a well-trained dog, but was of a reserved, suspicious character, refusing to associate with the other dogs, and showing no signs of affection towards its new master. There was a certain air of mystery about it, we used to say. It never barked, but kept a gloomy silence, as if it had been witness of scenes which it would rather not speak of. It wandered about at night. Bob must have been right in declaring that it had a bad conscience. It did not seem to care about life. A few weeks after it came to us, it allowed itself to be bitten by a snake; and though it got over this, it appeared to have become even more melancholy and meditative. At last one day it was not to be found, and we never saw it again. Desmond was sure it had committed suicide in the *laguna*.

CHAPTER XIII.

THE PLAGUES OF THE PAMPAS.

THERE was one great drawback to the enjoyment of my holiday on the Pampas. My friends, to whom it was no holiday, did not prosper in the *estancia* on which they had embarked all their means; and in this they were not worse off than the rest of their neighbours. The greatest industry and perseverance seemed hopelessly to struggle against fatal blunders made at starting, through inexperience and bad information. It turned out that the grass of these camps was not suitable for sheep. Cattle would do well, but so long as the settlers were not secure from Indian raids, they feared to invest their money in cattle, and in the number of horses required for working such an establishment, all of which might be driven away in a single night. Desmond and Eckford thought of selling their flock, and—as they afterwards did—turning their hands to agricultural farming, a kind of work both more toilsome and less profitable than sheep-breeding. Do what they would, their prospects were gloomy enough, and I wonder they could have been so cheerful, as they saw their hopes of soon returning to England with a competence disappear in the various train of losses and disappointments which came upon them almost weekly.

There was one enemy more destructive and less to be guarded against than even the Indians; I mean the locusts, who this year made a raid upon the country, after an absence of six or seven years, during which their room was signally preferred to their company. If you have never seen locusts, you will not appreciate my amazement when I first encountered a tribe of them blown in my face by the south wind as I rode along, and had to bend my head down while these enormous insects kept flopping against my face. And I remember Desmond's description of his first introduction to these insatiable pillagers. He was standing by the side of the house, talking to one of the *peons*, when something whizzed by his face and struck the wall behind him, so sharply that he looked to see who could be throwing anything at him; then another, and another, though there was no one in sight on the camp, and not a cloud in the sky.

'What's that?' he said to the *peon* in amazement, as they kept on pattering against the wall like gigantic raindrops.

'*Langostas! langostas!*' replied the *peon*, with more animation than was usual in him.

'*Que son langostas?*' asked Desmond innocently; but he was soon to know only too much about them. It was no matter for joking, though Bob Eckford, on hearing of these new acquaintances, remarked in his wonted vein—

'Locusts! Aren't they the beasts that make the wild honey?'

'Las Bischacheras' did not suffer so much from the locusts as some of the surrounding *estancias;* but the worst part of their work is that they keep the *estanciero* in a constant state of suspense. So long as they are about the country, he never knows whether, next day, a single green blade will be left him out of whatever crop he may have; and even if they do not eat the grass, they are said to poison it in some way, so as to make it unwholesome for the sheep.

One day great excitement was caused at the station by news that an army of locusts, myriads strong, was on its way to invade us. In our constant going and coming, a narrow straight track had been beaten down in the direction of Villa

Grande; and Bob, who had been out with the flock, rode back at full gallop to announce that this road was black with locusts, which, having taken it, probably, to avoid the trouble of pushing through the long grass, were not a quarter of a league off, coming with all speed to dine with us, as he expressed it with ill-timed facetiousness.

Immediately it was all hands to widen the ditch round our Indian corn. At this we worked desperately, and in the meanwhile threw out Seneccio as a picket to watch the movements of the enemy. He presently fell back, bringing a handful of them to show that he had actually been at close quarters, and his report was most alarming. They were still keeping the road that would bring them right upon us. Then Desmond went out, and brought back no better tidings. He described the locusts as appearing to have halted and massing themselves for the attack, while scouts ran up to the tops of the highest blades of grass, and seemed to be reconnoitring our position. The next news was that they were again bearing straight down upon us, and the anxiety of their unwilling hosts may be imagined. It now began to get dark, and nothing more could be done. Desmond and Eckford went to bed in a very bitter frame of mind; it was hard for them to resign themselves to the wholesale robbery of their property which was most likely going on without. The *peons* were very anxious to have the priest fetched, post haste, that he might lay a curse upon the locusts; but I am afraid Desmond, in his disgust, did a little of that work himself, and spoke very badly of locusts and priests, and South America in general. It was enough to make a saint swear.

In the morning, however, it was found that by some means or other the attention of the locusts had been diverted from the Indian corn, and that they, moreover, were gone. But they had fastened on a small patch of *alfalfa*, which they entirely stripped of its juicy blades, leaving nothing but a wilderness of dry stalks. Many a time had the horses and bullocks tried to break their way into this green enclosure; but when, that morning, they were allowed to have their will of it, they turned away sniffing and stamping, the very picture of disappointed expectation. But this was a small loss compared with the devastation which might have been effected. We heard of cases of whole districts, miles in extent, being laid waste as by a 'flame of fire that devoureth the stubble,'—fields, pastures, trees, and even the orchard, the pride of the *estancicro's* eye, which he had planted with his own hands, and watched for years, and successfully protected from the depredations of all other animals, made bare in a single night by these irre-

R

sistible invaders. 'The land is as the garden of Eden before them, and behind them as a desolate wilderness.'

These locusts lay or plant their eggs in cylindrical holes, which they generally make in places where the ground is hard and bare of grass. In a few weeks the young ones come up, and, I have been told, the first who appear begin their ravenous career a few minutes after birth by eating their younger brothers and sisters. If this be the case, it is a fine instance of the law of natural selection. The favoured first-born thrive so well on this cannibal diet, that they may almost be said to grow visibly, and soon gather strength to set out devouring and to devour. At first they travel on foot, and slowly; but the more they eat, the more lively they become, and their *crescendo* movement advances into a hop, at which stage they are most destructive, as having the vigorous appetite of youth and the capacious stomach of mature age. They increase thus, till they are the length of one's little finger; at last they take to flying I have seen them above me, in such numbers that they literally darkened the air like a thick cloud; and watching their steady flight, I pitied the *estanciero* within whose boundaries they should light down to take their evening meal. The cricket on the hearth is all very well; but members of the same tribe on the Pampas are among the most dreaded of plagues.

I don't know whether the hailstorms or the locusts should be counted as the greater calamity. Storms of all kinds are in this country extremely common and violent; but the occasional violence of the hailstorms is almost incredible to any one who has not witnessed their effects. I think I have not mentioned one such storm which occurred about a month after my arrival, and which was said to be the worst known for years. Of this storm I had an opportunity of judging for myself, which I ought not to recall without feeling thankful that I came out of it alive to report my experience.

Jim and one of the *peons* had gone with the bullock-cart to Villa Grande to fetch a load of wood, and in the course of the day I rode over with some letters for the mail. On the road I had expected to meet the cart returning, but could see nothing of it; and when I reached the *fonda*, I heard that Jim, to tell the plain truth, had got so drunk, that there was no likelihood of his being fit to bring the cart home that evening. I searched through the place, but could not find him. So, leaving my horse for his accommodation when he came to his senses, I set out with the *peon* on the cart, not altogether well pleased at exchanging the prospect of a good gallop home for the slow crawl of the bullocks; but to be candid, not wholly ill-pleased either, for my steed was an unsteady young animal, which had already given me a little trouble on the way to town. An ostrich starting up right under his nose, he swerved so suddenly as to make me lose my seat, and down I came, straining my shoulder, and exciting the contemptuous laughter of some natives who were witnesses of this catastrophe. A native, who on horseback is a kind of *centaur*, has no pity for a man that can't stick on the wildest animal in any emergency. My hurt, trifling as it was, made the bullock-cart not so undesirable as a means of conveyance on a hot afternoon. At all events, to this change I owed my escape from serious injuries, or worse.

When we were about half way home, we felt a sudden change in the temperature, and saw signs of a storm coming up to meet us.

'It's going to be wet,' said I sagely, fancying myself very weather-wise by this time.

'*Si, señor*,' replied the *peon*, who was my companion, lighting a fresh cigarette; and we took no further notice, except that I brought out my waterproof, in which, at my time of life, I rather enjoyed bidding defiance to the elements.

But, before long, we found that the storm which

was moving up to the attack, carried much heavier metal than a waterproof could be a defence against. As soon as the vanguard of the cloud came within range, as it were, a smart skirmishing fire was opened upon us in our exposed situation in the middle of the plain, with not a shred of shelter in sight.

'*Piedras, señor!*' cried the *peon;* for these are the only stones known in the district, and require no other description.

It was indeed *stones!* A long column of cloud was marching straight and swift upon us, and pouring out a volley of missiles, larger and thicker every moment.

We could not be careless now. In all haste we unyoked the bullocks, and fastened them under the lee of the cart, beneath which we then crept ourselves, not an instant too soon to escape serious injury from the hailstones. The *peon* showed me his hand bruised by one of them, and I had one or two black and blue marks on my face, though, in the excitement, I scarcely knew it at the time.

The storm soon raged around us with a fury of which it is impossible to give an adequate description. Most thankful we were to be thus under cover, when, between the peals of thunder, we heard the hail rattling on the cart like a constant discharge of musket-balls, and the poor bullocks lowing for fear and pain. I picked up three or four stones which, even after they had begun to melt, were larger than a walnut. It seemed as if no living thing could stand against such an artillery.

Fortunately it was soon over. But for about ten minutes these enormous hailstones kept pouring down; and when we ventured to emerge from our shelter, we found all the appearances of a battle-field. The bullocks were bleeding in several places, and trembling with fear. The ground was cut up as with balls, and a thick mist hung over it to the height of three or four feet, while the upper air was clear,—this phenomenon being caused, I suppose, by the melting hailstones affecting the temperature of the earth. As we followed for some distance along the track of the storm, we found the herbage bent and broken, and came upon several dead bodies of animals which had not been able to get out of the way of the missiles.

On arriving at the station, we were glad to find that it had not been touched. The limit of these storms is very partial; they go in strips, *mangas*, as the natives call them. A *manga de piedras*, literally, 'a sleeve or bag of stones,' is a thing by all means to be avoided, even though they be not so unusually large as on this occasion.

Our neighbours, however, were not so lucky. In

Villa Grande a woman and a child were killed outright on the *plaza*. Some parts of the town, I was told, looked as if they had just undergone a bombardment; and I afterwards saw round holes in tiles which the stones had gone through as clean as a bullet. A village some leagues off was almost entirely unroofed. A friend of ours had deadly slaughter made in his flock, chiefly among the lambs; and calves, also, were killed in many places. These cases I was able to verify; but I could add a long list of serious accidents and injuries which were reported to have happened, but which may have been inventions or exaggerations on the part of the natives.

When one has seen such storms as this, it is possible to understand what a 'plague of hail' may have been. But I doubt if any country is subject to such severe hailstorms as are common on the Pampas. Two or three years afterwards, Desmond wrote to me that a still more violent one had visited the district, during which hailstones had fallen that he was credibly informed weighed from eight to ten ounces. Nice weather to be out in, without an umbrella or a roof within a league of you! Fancy a shower of cricket balls!

Other plagues fell upon these unfortunate settlers that summer. Frogs, flies, and vermin might be said to be chronic afflictions of the country; now a murrain broke out among the cattle, a horrible complaint called *grano malo* by the natives, and so much dreaded by them, that when two of our bullocks died of it, no persuasion could induce the *peons* to assist in burying the bodies. The water round about was turned, not indeed into blood, but into salt, the heat of the sun drying up the *lagunas*, and leaving in their beds a deposit of saline mud, which from a distance seemed white as snow. In addition, there were rumours of the cholera having broken out in some parts of the country; and, what terrified the natives more than anything else, we were visited for a few minutes by a plague of partial darkness, through an eclipse of the sun, which did not affect us Englishmen much, but by our *peons* was connected with the other troubles, and ascribed to supernatural interference with the order of things.

So it was no wonder if an ignorant and fanatical priest at Villa Grande made a great sensation among his hearers by a sermon preached during Lent, in which he announced that the country was actually being chastised by the very plagues of Egypt, as a judgment for having allowed the introduction of Protestants and Bibles! If there were any judgment in the matter, he would have been nearer the mark if he had set it down to the impiety of his flock, the male members of which generally spent Sunday morning at a cock-fight while their wives were at church; or he might have put on sackcloth and ashes for his own shortcoming in the way of cheating at cards, which was so much his reputation that one believed there must be something in it. Desmond declared he had caught him in the act; but Desmond, being a very zealous Irish Protestant, is not to be taken as an unprejudiced witness against a Catholic.

Of us three this priest had an especial horror. He once paid us a visit, and told us a wonderful story about an image of the Virgin Mary which had been found among a tribe of savage Indians, and had clearly come there, he inferred, by miraculous agency. Eckford, like a hard-headed Scotchman, refused to take this view of the case, and suggested that the image had probably come into possession of the Indians through much more credible and discreditable means, the plunder of a church, to wit, a thing which had often happened in old days. At this the priest waxed hot, and finally flung out of our house in a rage, cursing and swearing at us, as Bob said, like a madman. Desmond would have it that the real reason of his sudden departure was that he found we were not going to offer him any spirits. I should be sorry to offend any one's religious prejudices, but the plain truth is, as every candid and sensible person acquainted with the people knows, that it would be difficult to exaggerate the ignorance and worthlessness of the Roman Catholic priesthood of this country, which owes to their influence so much of its misfortunes.

Even pious and well-meaning Catholics were superstitious enough to mistrust us, and to blame sometimes the tolerant spirit of their Government towards the heretics. We, of course, did not attribute our want of prosperity to any special interference of providence, but to the exceptional badness of the year, and to the fact of our having been ill advised, or sometimes, to put it bluntly, *cheated*, as to the selection of a locality. But, from whatever cause it arose, the distress among some of the settlers was very great. Many of our neighbours found themselves unable to indulge in any luxuries; their food was beef and biscuits, and even *yerba* and tobacco had to be given up or strictly economized. There was one *estancia* we knew of, where the owners of leagues of land could not even afford beef, but lived for weeks upon stinted rations of plain biscuit, except when they were able to shoot some beast or bird, and for that they had to borrow powder.

My adventurous young readers must not suppose

that I am writing to discourage them from emigrating to the Pampas or elsewhere, but only to bid them look well before taking such a long leap. I am speaking of a district which has not, as yet, turned out well; but it must be remembered that, if there were many difficulties to overcome, land was comparatively cheap, also that good fortunes have been made in this country, and are still to be made if the business be rightly undertaken, and a better state of political affairs gives a fair chance to the peaceable and industrious settler.

There are thousands of young men in England who could do better for themselves by emigrating; and thousands of those who emigrate would have done better if they had shown more consideration in looking about and choosing their ground and the manner of their operations, instead of being in too great a hurry to set up for themselves, and become rich, as they hoped, all at once. Everything takes time and experience. Every part of the world has its advantages and disadvantages; and the kind of life on which one man would thrive and grow fat, would be nothing but weariness and leanness of spirit to another. Riches, as a rule, are not got off-hand; the Eldorado of which imaginative youth has dreamed, turns out generally to be a very prosaic land, where the gold and silver are slow to come upon, and take a great deal of hard and dirty work, before they can be picked out of the earth. But in most countries there is as much of these metals to be found as in any other, if you have a turn for the work that is wanted, and will learn how to set about it. Then, though a good man may sometimes be unfortunate for a time, in the long run it will seldom happen that honest labour and prudent forethought fail to reap their reward.

My wonder is not that so many fail, but that so many succeed out of such communities as are generally to be found in a new colony. There is a large class of settlers who don't get on abroad, just as they would not have got on at home, having left their native country because they could not, or would not, work there, and being foolish enough to imagine that nature is more indulgent to uselessness or idleness elsewhere. Every settlement like that I am describing is full of such failures,—men who only leave the restraining influences of home and society, to fall deeper and deeper into ruin and degradation, as what else could be expected of them? Too many of these sad cases did I see, even among the stations immediately round us! And, in nine instances out of ten, it is drink that is the beginning and the end of it. Drink, so deadly in England, is doubly the curse of colonial life, in which all classes of settlers are tempted to this indulgence by the monotony and drudgery of farm work, and the absence of counteracting influences to elevate the tone and refine the habits of society.

I came across one very sad example of this, in the case of an old schoolfellow of my own, the son of a baronet, who, as a boy, had been a universal favourite, and shown great promise of talent. I knew he was in the country somewhere, for I had seen two of his old prize books exposed for sale at a store in Villa Grande, kept by a German Jew, who carried on a trade very like that of a pawnbroker for the surrounding camps. But I was rather surprised when I found my old friend acting as stoker on the railway. Soon afterwards an accident happened through his fault while in a state of intoxication, and he had to leave even this distasteful employment, with no prospect or desire of getting any other. He came out to the station to visit us; but he was in such a state of filth and neglect, that Bob Eckford insisted on himself and his clothes being well washed before he was allowed to enter the house. He did not stay long with us; and some time afterwards I heard that he had died of *delirium tremens.*

I don't care to preach, though in this matter

preaching is no sure sign of moral superiority. I never was more feelingly and earnestly warned against the dangers of drink than by an American of good position, who, I afterwards heard, was himself one of the greatest drunkards in the country. He had not so far lost his wits as to be ignorant of what is really meant when men cant about the 'cheerful glass' and the 'jovial bowl.' And, seeing what I have seen, I can't help speaking plainly what every sensible man must know to be true. Let all young fellows who have the enterprise to think of emigrating to the colonies, first settle in their own minds whether they have enough manliness to go through toils and hardships without giving way to the habit of making beasts of themselves; and even though they be strong in self-confidence and good resolutions, let them remember well how many bright and hopeful lives have been corrupted and wasted by this terriblest of plagues which the English race seems cursed to carry with it into every quarter of the globe.

CHAPTER XIV.

CARNIVAL AMUSEMENTS.

SOON after the expedition against the Indians, Desmond went to Cordova, the capital of the province, on business which kept him away about a fortnight. I was to have gone with him, but was prevented by an annoying accident, which may look like a very insignificant one. A black ant stung me on the ankle, and some dirt getting into the puncture, my foot swelled and festered so much that I was scarcely able to put it to the ground.

I was sorry I did not visit Cordova, since Desmond described it as a very handsome town, sheltered by picturesque mountains, full of fine churches, tall poplar trees, gardens, and streams of running water in the streets. I should also much like to have seen and been able to describe the Carnival, which took place during his visit; but I must content my readers by Desmond's account of it, extracted from a letter he wrote to us, which, by the way, we did not receive till after his return,—the explanation of this delay being, that the man in charge of the mails had a sweetheart at Villa Nueva, one of the stations on the line; and he having gone off to visit her, the train left without him. So we did not require to read my cousin's letter at the time; but here it is in my desk, and this is what he says about the national and unrational amusements of the Carnival:

'I went out yesterday afternoon in my waterproof coat and a pair of old pants, and I hadn't got to the corner of the street before I was cooled externally, and my temper was heated, by a bucket of water thrown over me from the top of one of the houses, where I could see an ugly old woman peeping over the wall and grinning at the effect of her salute. This made me more careful, and I dodged along safely till I came to the principal streets. At first sight, the town seemed to have become a city of the dead. There were almost no foot-passengers, and you might look all the way along the streets, square after square, without seeing a single vehicle. But as I was wondering what had become of the people, suddenly I heard a burst of laughter from a balcony, and saw a row of ladies preparing to assault me with eggs.

'"*Sombrero! Sombrero!*" they cried; and before I could run for it, one of them knocked off my hat with a well-directed shot, and another egg, full of perfumed water, was smashed right between my eyes.

'I wasn't able to return these compliments; but now the ladies were going to meet their match. Up rattled a carriage full of young fellows in fancy dresses, and loaded with bouquets, bonbons, eggs, and other missiles. They pulled up

THE CARNIVAL.—*The Pampas*, p. 272.

before the balcony, and at once opened fire. Now came a lively fight. The girls, who had their faces protected by masks, poured eggs and jokes upon the men in the carriage, while they kept flinging up flowers and sweetmeats, half of which fell short of the mark, and were scrambled for by a lot of ragged imps who appeared suddenly from nobody knows where, as soon as there was anything to be picked up.

'After looking on for a little, I made a dash to get to Hemming's office. But I had to run the gauntlet of all sorts of missiles, handfuls of flour and peas, showers of water from the roofs, paper bags full of water, aimed to burst on your head, eggs going squash, squash all round you, and roars of laughter following each successful shot. At one corner, some fellows were keeping up a continuous stream of water from a sort of fire-engine. I confess I didn't altogether see the fun of this sort of thing. It is all very well to be peppered with eggs by a pretty girl in a balcony; but to be drenched with a can full of water by a sneaking urchin behind a door, or get a smash on the nose from some clumsy brute of a man, is a kind of a joke that not even an Irishman can understand.

'At last I got to Hemming and Co.'s office, and joined the clerks in an egg fight with two dark-eyed beauties on the top of the opposite house. If Eckford had been there, or any other Scotchman, he would have said it was rather an expensive kind of game. The eggs cost about tenpence a dozen, and a dozen won't last long at this sort of work. There must have been a good deal of money spent on eggs, for the streets are quite covered with the pieces. I daresay we could easily throw away our *estancia* in this way, and not take many days about it either. It goes on for three days.

'The police have made regulations for keeping the row within due bounds. All persons wishing to play the tomfool or wear masks have to register their names and addresses, and take out a licence. The fun has to begin at two, and to

S

be over by sundown, a gun being fired as a signal at each of these hours. Nothing is to be thrown more dangerous than water or common eggs (*ostrich* eggs are prohibited) filled with perfumed water. No arms are to be carried. But, in spite of these precautions, they say there are generally a good many rows, and a murder or two.

'I saw one rather serious accident. As I was going back with some fellows, we saw a stuffed figure hanging in the middle of the street, held up by ropes from the houses on each side. Some of us proposed to cut it down, for a lark; but just as two of the fellows had got out their knives, a bell was rung, something was shouted at us through a speaking-trumpet, and down came the figure upon our heads with more force than we had bargained for. I got hold of it by the waist, but the rope was too thick to be cut in a hurry, and I was obliged to let go, or I should have been hauled up by the men in the house who were managing the trick. We were glad to get off so easily, for we saw afterwards that the figure was so heavy, and was whipped about so skilfully, that two or three people were knocked over as they passed below, to the great delight of the crowd which had gathered to watch this amusement. After a little a water-cart came by, and when the figure was let down upon it, the ropes got entangled in the wheels of the cart. The driver whipped up his horse and drove ahead, and it ended in one of the balconies above giving way, and three men in it fell into the street and were hurt, one of them badly. They thought he was dead. Of course this stopped the fun, and when the police came, the poor fellow who was driving the cart was arrested and taken to prison, as if it was his fault. They do things in a peculiar way in this country. Two men were stabbed in the streets last night, and the police have them both in charge,—one dead and one nearly so; but nobody knows what has become of the murderers.'

While Desmond was thus absent on *business*, Bob Eckford and I felt like the Welsh lady in the story, who, when her husband had gone to a fox-hunt, declared that it wasn't fair that he alone should be enjoying himself, and sent out to ask if there wasn't a *funeral* or other amusement going on anywhere in the neighbourhood. On making inquiries, we learned there were to be races at Villa Grande on the last day of the Carnival; and as my foot was now much better, we resolved to 'assist' at this entertainment.

The races began at two o'clock, upon an open space just out of the town. The scene, as may be supposed, was a gay one, every one of the crowd of natives being attired in his most gorgeous costume. Whom should we find here but our friend the Italian organ-grinder, as lively and good-natured as ever, and making a very good day's work of it among the delighted and astonished *gauchos!* Some of the horses were well worth seeing; I felt quite ashamed of the lean, stumbling steed which I bestrode for want of a better, and about which the Commandante, wishing to be complimentary, but scarcely knowing which point to select for praise, without his politeness becoming mere irony, made this significant remark, 'He has a fine tail!'

That was all that could be said for him. But

Bob was well mounted on a fine black horse, which he would have liked very well to try against one of the natives' horses, if they would have consented to a fair trial over a good space of ground, without any of the absurd preliminary ceremonies which are the custom.

The horses run bare-backed and in pairs. The rule is to allow sixteen, or even more, false starts, at the option of the riders. They come up slowly to the starting-point, and one holds up his whip, and cries out a challenge, which the other either accepts by replying '*Bueno!*' and they are off, or more likely declines, when both dismount and lead their horses slowly back. In this way we saw nearly an hour wasted over a race which, after all, was only over two squares, *i.e.* 300 yards. The object of this is to excite the horses; and it must be a very steady horse which is able to preserve its *equinimity*—this was Eckford's little joke—in such circumstances. Then, when they have started, it is another 'custom of the country' for one rider, if he can, to kick his opponent's horse in the chest,—a trick which, if well managed, may decide the race; and, naturally, a race so decided often ends in a scene of quarrelling and brawling, so that racing on the Pampas is even a less moral form of amusement than at home.

There were also going on some of the native games on horseback. One was, tilting at a ring, which had to be carried away by men riding at full speed. In another, the *gauchos* formed themselves into two lines, and endeavoured to lasso the horse of one of their comrades who ran the gauntlet between them, but seldom got far without being overthrown. The organ-grinder stood by playing a lively strain, and one might have thought that it was the good old English dance of the 'Haymakers' being performed on horseback.

But it was very hot and dusty, and I had a headache, so I did not take much interest in these sports. The Commandante, who, after our exploit against the Indians, was inclined to be very civil, asked us to a party, not indeed to dine, but to come in the evening for *maté*, and it seemed desirable to take a rest before this festivity. We left the racecourse early, and went off to dine at the *fonda* before it should become too crowded. As it was, the place was uncomfortably full of natives, who, in hot weather, are apt to 'come out strong' in a sense which Mark Tapley did not contemplate.

Opposite us, at the table, sat a good-looking young fellow apparently of the better class of native *estancieros*, who seemed to take great interest in our conversation, and frequently looked as if he were about to address us. We did not, however, suppose that he could understand our language, until, to our amazement, he said slowly and distinctly—

'Wull ye han' the breid, please?'

'Do you speak English?'

'Ou ay,' he answered, in broad Scotch tones, slightly modified by a foreign accent, and forming a most ludicrous contrast to the extreme politeness of his manner; 'Ma feyther cam frae Auchterarder. Are ye acquaint wi' it?'

We could scarcely help bursting out laughing; but a little further conversation cleared up the puzzle. Our new acquaintance's name was Don Juan Macwhannel. His father was a Scotch shepherd, who had emigrated nearly thirty years before, and was doing very well in a part of the Banda Oriental where there were no other European settlers. The worthy shepherd and his wife had done their best to bring up the family in their own tongue, as a proof of which the son informed us that he could say the whole of the *Shorter Catechism* by heart; but he confessed that he was much more at home in Spanish than in speaking the ancestral language, which he innocently and proudly took for pure English. Being born in the country, he was liable to serve in the army, and after being ordered several times to present himself for this purpose, a band of soldiers was at last sent to enlist him *nolens volens;* and he had escaped by mounting a fine horse and riding forty leagues before sunset. He was now a refugee in the Argentine States, and did not mean to return, unless some arrangement could be made for his exemption from service. His father and mother spoke of selling off and returning to end their days in their native country, which the old pair, so long absent from it, would probably revisit with as much bewilderment as a couple of Rip van Winkles.

Bob Eckford was delighted to fall in with a fellow-countryman, and, in the off-hand way of the camp, gave Don Juan an invitation to come and spend some time at our *estancia.* So it was arranged that he should ride home with us that night, and make himself generally useful, like the rest of the family, till he or they were tired of the arrangement.

But first we had to keep our engagement at the Commandante's, where we found a large party hard at work playing *lotteria* and *monte.* We were most affably received by the ladies of the family, who were very pretty and very fat, and who played cards with us, and won more money from us than I liked, with the greatest politeness in the world. Only, one couldn't help being just a little surprised when the mistress of the house rose from the table, and proceeded to—in fact, to give her baby its supper, in full view of all the company, one of whom, I can answer for it, modestly looked the other way.

Every country has its own customs; and now, with all my four months' experience of the manners of good Argentine society, I was very nearly falling into one of the snares which Spanish etiquette sets for the unwary foreigner. I happened to admire a singularly well-carved gourd and *bombilla* in which *maté* was served to me; and on expressing my admiration to the host, he at once, as their way is, begged me to consider it at my disposal.

'Oh no! I couldn't think of taking it,' I declared, knowing that this was only a very usual compliment; but the Commandante insisted, pressing the gift upon me so hard, that I was at a loss how to refuse; and in the end, fairly deceived by his assurances that he could have no greater pleasure than to know that I accepted his present, I had almost done so, when Bob gave me a great kick under the table, as a hint to mind what I was about. The Commandante expressed himself as much concerned that I would not take him at his word; but if I had done so, he would have looked as black as thunder, for the *maté* apparatus must have been a valuable piece of work, and was perhaps an heirloom.

We were shown another curiosity that I must not omit to mention—the fossil shell of an enormous armadillo which had lately been found in the river-bed, and was to be sent to a museum at Buenos Ayres. It must have been at least a yard and a half long, and was in almost perfect preservation. Such remains are very common in this country. We often picked up fragments of bones that had belonged to even larger animals.

After taking leave of the Commandante and his friends, we turned in for a few minutes to see a ball at which the lower class of the natives were amusing themselves. This entertainment was going on in a long low room, rather feebly lit by guttering tallow candles, round the walls of which the guests sat or stood, and watched a single couple moving gravely to the music of guitars. The dance was very slow and stately, and set off well the dignity of the native manners; but I could see very little fun in it, till Bob Eckford stood up with a barefooted, black-eyed beauty, and insisted on trying his hand, or rather his foot. Then nobody could help laughing, to see the heavy, awkward way in which he endeavoured to imitate the graceful movements of his partner; but at last, giving it up as a bad job, broke out into a step that looked like a cross between the hornpipe and the Highland fling.

There was another dance which was gone through with castanets, and after that came a handkerchief-dance, which was really very pretty to look at. But we were too tired to wait long, and left the ballroom just as a certain air of liveliness seemed to be breaking out among the party, and the music struck up a polka mazurka, while the cavaliers gallantly began to ply their partners with the refreshments of the evening, gin and *maté*.

At the corner of the street we came upon another 'custom of the country,' unfortunately too common, especially at Carnival time and other festive seasons. A little crowd had gathered, in the midst of which we heard a sound of brawling and screaming, and the clash of knives. One or two of these men were dressed more or less grotesquely in a provincial attempt at masquerading; but this was evidently a tragedy rather than a comedy that was being acted, and peeping over the heads of the mob, we could see the plot at a glance. On one side stood a tall mulatto, looking furious, and brandishing his knife; on the other, a slim young fellow, with a paper fool's cap on his head, had fallen back into the arms of a pretty girl, who was invoking the Virgin and the crowd alternately, shrieking to her lover's assailant to stand off, and stanching with her scarf the blood that poured from the wounded man's side. It was a horrible sight, the poor fellow's face white with rage and pain, and his hand clutching eagerly in the air, as if seeking the knife, which had fallen to the ground. I was indignant, and proposed to Eckford that we should run in and interfere, as the mulatto seemed inclined to finish his murderous work.

'No use,' whispered my cautious friend. 'It's ten to one if we could do any good, and it's twenty to one that we shouldn't have one of these knives in our own ribs. See, the crowd are separating them; and here come the soldiers! We had best be off, or we shall be dragged into the row, somehow or other.'

Indeed, just then, the murderer saw fit to disappear, and there was no want of help for his victim. So we turned away, and made towards the *fonda* where our horses were, agreeing that people who get drunk and lose their temper shouldn't be allowed to carry knives, as these *gauchos* do.

As we crossed the *plaza*, we saw a number of noisy and ragged urchins, who were burning an effigy of Judas Iscariot with the same pious zeal with which boys at home are accustomed to testify to their orthodoxy by making Guy Fawkes the excuse for smoke and mischief—Guy Fawkes, who here would be a martyr, or a saint, for all I know, if the natives had ever heard of him. Such are the antipodes of human sentiments!

At the *fonda* we met our new friend Don Juan, and all three of us were not long of saddling and being off. We rode along, chatting pleasantly in the moonlight upon the manners and customs of this country; but when we had left the town some league or so behind, we were aware of a small band of horsemen riding after us at full gallop, and shouting to us to stop.

'Hallo! they are following us, surely,' said Eckford, reining in his horse and looking round.

'What ails them at us?' asked Don Juan Macwhannel, looking to his girths like a man who knew what it was to ride for life or liberty.

'Best wait,' was Bob's opinion. 'No use tiring our horses.'

So we all pulled up, and waited for the pursuers, rather puzzled to account for the haste with which they were riding at that time of night. Something serious must have happened. It crossed my mind that perhaps we were wanted as witnesses of the stabbing case. Then it occurred to me that our companion might be a bad character, who was 'wanted.' I vainly taxed my memory to think of any way in which Bob or I could have offended against the laws of this enlightened country. Was it possible that the Commandante's *maté* gourd was missing, and that he suspected us of taking it away in our sacks, like Joseph's brethren? But we should soon know all about it; for now the riders were near enough to let us recognise them as a part of our late host's ragged warriors, and we could see one of them waving a hat in the air with excited gestures.

When at last they came up to us, one word explained the whole matter, and set us off into a roar of laughter. I had taken away the Commandante's hat by mistake, instead of my own—that was all; and here it was, sent after me in hot haste, escorted by a detachment of the Argentine army. Was an old felt hat ever so honoured before?

The exchange was soon made; the soldiers were rewarded for their trouble by thanks, and by more substantial marks of gratitude, such as require no foreign language for their expression; with profuse politeness they took leave of us; and we turned our horses' heads once more towards home, which we reached soon after midnight, and went straight to bed, thinking that a festival day, with all its amusement, was rather a dull affair, so far as we were concerned.

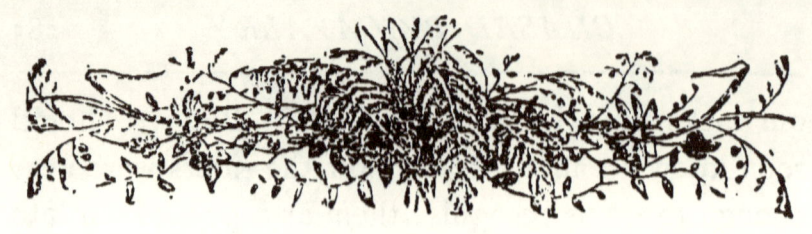

CHAPTER XV.

A CAMP FIRE.

WE were now coming to April, 'that sweet and jolly time,' as many an old and new poet has sung, 'when little herbs shoot forth, and the meadows grow green again, and all the plants are longing to be in flower.' But far other were the signs of April in this southern world, where the grass was now long and coarse, the gay flowers had withered, and the bare patches round the *bis-cacho* burrows let us see the extraordinary little heaps of rubbish which these creatures delight in accumulating at the mouth of their holes. At night, sometimes, there was a touch of frost, though through the day the sun was as hot as in an English summer. Where there are few trees, and most of these evergreens, and where the skies are almost always cloudless, the changes of the seasons are only indicated by such marks as these.

But I for one marked the flight of time with no indifferent eye, for soon this pleasant holiday of mine was to come to an end, and it behoved me to return to England, with its hawthorns and daisies, its fogs and drizzles.

My original plan had been to sail from Buenos Ayres at the end of the month. But on the first of April I discovered a bunch of letters in the wick of the candle, and this augury turned out not to be making a fool of me ; for next day, sure enough, the letters came to hand, and I was somewhat ill pleased to find from one of them that it was desirable that I should return without delay. What must be, must be, however ; so my luggage was despatched by the next bullock-cart to the station at Villa Grande, and it was settled that four days afterwards I should set off, so as to get to Buenos Ayres in time to catch the first steamer. These days passed away only too quickly, and my last night on the Pampas arrived.

Darrell came over to spend the evening with us, accompanied by his two sons, black-eyed, tawny-skinned, lithe-limbed youngsters, who could ride or throw a lasso as well as any *gaucho*, and were more familiar with Spanish than English. Their mother was a native woman. The elder of them was seventeen, and having been born in the country, they would soon be liable to service in the army,—no pleasant prospect, especially as there were rumours of another revolutionary war, brought about by disputes in which the settlers had not the least interest. So their father had some notion of sending them to England soon, and wished me to make inquiries about a suitable school, which I promised to do, though I could not help inwardly pitying the lot of these unbroken young colts if subjected to the restraints of an English school.

Our visitors, having a long way to go home, left us early, and we sat talking for an hour or two over a fire of maize cobs. Though it was our last night together, we did not forget that we had to be up early in the morning, and in good time retired to rest.

My friends were soon asleep, but I lay awake for an hour or so, thinking over the new experiences of life which I had acquired during the past five months, and wondering how I should feel on returning to the land of high hats and kid gloves. And just as I was turning round for the last time, and, mindful of the long journey before me, was about to close my eyes, and go resolutely to sleep, I was startled by a gleam of light through the slit in the wall opposite my bed. I sat up, I rubbed my eyes; but there could be no doubt about it. There was a bright blaze outside, and now the dogs were beginning to bark loudly, as if to call our attention.

·I leaped to my feet and ran to the door, calling out to Desmond and Eckford, as I fumbled with the rough bolt, for the evening had been chilly enough to persuade us to shut ourselves in. In a moment I stood shivering outside, and what a sight met my eyes!

The whole plain to the south seemed to be a sheet of flame, sending up a lurid glare, and covering one side of the sky with a copper-coloured glow. This vast stretch of fire, spreading steadily on either hand, was sweeping straight towards us, and seemed already close to the house, though it was in reality many miles away. But the fresh wind which blew right in our faces told us that before long the conflagration would be brought to our door.

For the moment, there was no thought of peril in my mind; the grandeur of the spectacle overpowered everything else. My friends, however, who had seen such sights too often, and whose property was in danger, were not inclined to take the picturesque view of the matter.

'The camp on fire!' said Bob Eckford, and deliberately retired to put on his clothes, while Desmond, who did not take things so coolly, rushed off to waken the sleepy-headed *peons;* Senecio was already awake and grinning. Then I began to be aware that the night was cold, and ran in-doors to put on my clothes as hastily as possible.

'What a lucky thing that we thought of clearing away the grass all round the house!' said Eckford. 'At this time of the year there is sure to be a fire somewhere about. But it won't go much farther. There was a fire on Clarke's camp the other night, you know; everything is burned up there, and that will stop it.'

Luckily, as he said, a wide clearing had been made round our house, and inside the ditch there was nothing to burn except a patch of Indian corn, just ready for gathering. The iron roof of the house, too, was a great safeguard; there was nothing about it which could be set on fire by sparks or burning fragments. But, none the less, it was necessary to take all precautions, and soon every one about the place was busy filling buckets of water, wetting the posts of the *corral*, and covering the reed thatch of the sheds with wet sheepskins, while others were put ready to beat out the fire if it should cross our ditch. Three or four horses, turned into the *corral* to be at hand next morning, were tied fast to the posts of the *ramada*, and the bullock-cart, which stood a short distance out among the grass, was hauled up under the lee of the buildings.

These arrangements made, we got on the roof of the house, and, lighting our cigarettes, watched the progress of the fire, which was now about half a league off. As we calculated, it stretched across not less than twelve miles of the camp, bending outwards, so as to form a convex semicircle, terrible as the bow of Achilles—so Desmond said, with a very vague reminiscence of Homer's *Iliad*. But there was no noise, except the occasional cries of animals frightened from their haunts, strangely breaking in upon the stillness which added to the awe of the scene. Steadily and silently the wall of flame, edged with light glowing smoke, moved forward, here and there darkened by a rolling volume of thicker smoke, that marked where a small *laguna* was forcing it to turn and creep slowly round its damp edges, and the fire was hissing and struggling among beds of rank reeds. The light was now bright enough to read by; the smoke was already blowing in our faces, and every minute we caught sight of deer or ostriches bounding by, flying from the fury of the resistless flames. Our horses, following the trotting and lowing bullocks, had some time before galloped away to the other side of the camp at a speed which promised a hard morning's work to whoever should have to find and bring them back.

Suddenly Desmond, prowling about to see that

nothing had been forgotten, found a weak point in our defences. Part of the ditch had become overgrown with grass and weeds, which might serve to carry the foe across among the Indian corn, the very thing most liable to catch fire, now that it was full-grown and dry. So we had all to exert ourselves, and, as well as possible in the short time that remained, set to work dragging out this grass, and piling it up at one end near the well, where water could be poured over it, and where, if it did catch fire, the wind would blow it harmlessly away. We all worked with a will; even the lazy *peons* became excited, and actually threw away their cigarettes. We performed prodigies, and in ten minutes had cleared out a great part of the ditch, on the side from which the flames were approaching. But before we could finish the task the fire was upon us.

Now came a short space of confusion and wild excitement, during which we, half a dozen men, cut off from the rest of the world, scarcely drew our breath in the midst of this deluge of flame, and struggled against the power that seemed about to sweep us away with it. Whichever way we turned our eyes, we were dazzled with the glare, and the heat and smoke almost choked us. The air was full of sparks, handfuls of burning grass were blown in our faces, while the perspiration streamed from every pore, as we rushed here and there with wet sheepskins in our hands, and dashed upon every blaze that leapt up within the ditch. Mingled with the dull steady crackling of the fire, rose the frightened bleating of the sheep in the *corral*, and the neighing of the horses trying to break loose from the posts to which they had been tied, and the shouts of the men calling to each other for assistance against some new outbreak of the fire. Again and again it jumped over the ditch and spluttered within the enclosure; every time we beat it out; each of us seemed to be three men at once; we flew from spot to spot; not a moment's rest, though the smoke grew thicker and the heat more intolerable every moment.

The pile of grass catches; we hurl it down; the flames are extinguished—no, they rise from the other side; we must leave it, for the Indian corn has caught—we fling ourselves upon it in a body; we beat down the flames, raising clouds of sparks. Now comes the real struggle! The fire has crossed among the Indian corn at half a dozen points; we have already extinguished it as often; we scarcely feel the sparks and the heat; panting, we rush from place to place. In vain we crush out the invading element—as each blaze disappears, another smouldering seed bursts out; the tongues of flame leap higher, and fly towards each other through the tall dry stalks of the corn;

they unite, they advance with an angry crackle; a small line of flame is formed and sweeps on, sending out in front little skirmishing blazes which spread round with too great rapidity to be longer checked. We follow; we attack the main body of this foe; but we might as well try to bridle the wind. New flames start up on every side; we can do no more. Senecio is howling from the pain of a burned arm, and nobody has time to console him. Desmond falls, almost fainting from exhaustion; we draw him back to the side where the fire is already burned out, and, acknowledging our defeat, watch the flame have its will of the Indian corn, and sputter harmlessly here and there through the short and scanty grass of the enclosure.

The danger was over now. Three minutes were enough for the fire to lick up the Indian corn with a corner of its tongue, as it were, and now the whole body of it had passed by the *estancia*, and was rolling away through the plain of long dry grass, leaving behind a wilderness of stifling smoke and smouldering ashes.

Nothing more could be done except to attend to Senecio's arm, which, after all, was not so much hurt, and to refresh ourselves with a *maté* all round after our exertions, then go to bed to get as much sleep as possible in what was left of the night. The morning would bring its own evils—horses and bullocks several hours' journey off, the pasture burned up for miles around, nothing to be seen of the little crop of corn and vegetables but ashes and charred stalks. It was enough to make me pity my friends whom I was leaving behind in such misfortune; but for their part, they accepted it philosophically enough, as one of the ordinary incidents of a settler's life. I wondered how they could take it so coolly, but my concern on their account did not prevent me from dropping off to sleep at last. And thus strangely passed my last night on the Pampas.

We were all up betimes next morning, and out to look at the burned camp. A strange sight it was, to see the ground all black and bare as far as the eye could reach, while the brilliant blue sky seemed to mock the desolation below. There was not a trace of the fire in the horizon; it had burned itself out, and the air, that a few hours before had been filled with smoke and ashes, was now clear and balmy.

But there was little time for attending to the poetic aspects of the scene. Both my friends had their hands full at home that morning. I was bound to ride to Villa Grande to catch the first train, and they had intended to accompany me so far; but now they must look after their hungry and thirsty animals, so I would have to ride into the town alone, leaving my horse at the *fonda* till they could send for it. The *peons* had started at daybreak to bring in the strayed horses, but had not yet returned.

Our parting was somewhat hasty, then; and perhaps this was just as well, for we were all sorry to part, and, like true Britons, did not care to show it. But Senecio was not to be restrained from a demonstrative exhibition of grief; he cried noisily in a way which was very like laughing, and professed the bitterest regret that he was to see me no more. I believe the young rogue was delighted at the bottom of his heart, as I comforted him by a present of some coarse red handkerchiefs which I had brought for use in camp, to save washing, and which he, no doubt, regarded as a highly ornamental addition to his wearing apparel.

So, with tears, real or feigned, on Senecio's part, and hearty hand-shakings and warm good-byes and kind messages to all friends at home from Desmond and Eckford, I mounted my horse, which, being an impulsive, inconsiderate animal, cut short all further leave-taking by plunging forward almost before I was on its back. We all gave a great shout, and I was off for England. But I kept turning round and waving my hand to my friends, as they stood smoking their cigarettes and watching me till horse and man could scarcely be distinguished; and when I came to a place where there was a slight dip in the ground, I stopped to take one more look at the house and *corral*, and could still see Bob Eckford's tall figure as he rounded up the sheep which had just been let out. Then I no longer curbed the impatience of my hard-mouthed steed, but set off at a good pace, enjoying my last gallop on the Pampas.

Before long I came to the limits of the fire, which had stopped on meeting a tract of ground burned a short time before. And this, which had lately looked so dry, now seemed flourishing in comparison with the desert over which I had just passed. It was a consolation to think that the grass would soon spring up from the ashes, all the more green and luxurious for this wholesome destruction. But I wished I could have left 'Las Biscacheras' in a more flourishing state.

CHAPTER XVI.

CONCLUSION.

AM now going to conclude by a few rough notes, from my diary, of the journey to Buenos Ayres. In my eagerness to take him out at once with me on the Pampas, the reader was spared a good deal of introductory description; so he must not yet expect to see the last of me when I parted from my friends and set out for the railway station.

It seemed like the first taste of civilised life, having to take care not to lose a train. In good time, however, I found myself on the platform of the little station, and duly embarked on the train for Rosario. It was a splendid day, and I had all the will in the world to keep my eyes open along the route; but I was tired after my exertions of the night before, and had a slight headache, so all I can remember of this part of this journey, is that

I dozed in a corner of the car and felt uncomfortable in this once familiar mode of transit.

The train went slowly along, but late in the afternoon we arrived at Rosario, and I made my way to an uncomfortable hotel with a pretentious name, where I once more had the opportunity of enjoying some of the luxuries of polite life. There was a real dining-room, a square, white-washed apartment, in the middle of which stood a large mahogany table on civilised legs, and round the wall respectable chairs, and an actual sofa with stuffed and knobby cushions. The wall was also ornamented with coarse engravings of Napoleon Bonaparte, Garibaldi, and General Mitre, one of the national celebrities. But the chief wonder was the fire-place, a mongrel sort of affair, something between an open grate and a close stove; still it was a real fire-place. In this scene of magnificence I was served by a waiter, a dirty but good-natured Italian, in his shirt sleeves, and was treated to a dinner of fish, beef stewed with mushrooms, and chocolate ices. Truly I had passed the border line of romance; my half-year's picnic on the Pampas was over.

After dinner I strolled about the town, which is clearly a rising place. Merchants' offices and warehouses are elbowing out the old low houses with their pleasant gardens, and in the streets European costumes are largely mixed with the national attire, as well as with the scanty and nondescript rags of young urchins gambolling in the middle of the carriage-way. I saw one or two cafés and other marks of progress, which indeed comes easy to Rosario, as it is quite a modern town created by the demands of foreign trade. Something is still to be desired, however, in the matter of pavement; some of the streets looked as if they would be impassable in wet weather. The tradesmen seemed to be particularly fond of signs. Looking along a street, one could see a row of miscellaneous articles, such as gilded sheep, huge boots, hats, miniature coffins, and so forth.

About midnight I embarked on board the *Pavon*, a small steamboat, which looked just like those which ply on the Clyde, and, as likely as not, had come from that locality. Anyhow, the engineer was a Scotchman—of course. Later on, he and I made friends, and he took me into his cabin, treated me to bottled beer, and told me many stories of the late war between Buenos Ayres and the other Argentine States, in the navy of which latter he had occupied a distinguished position, but had left it in consequence of getting no pay.

The saloon was crowded with people, sleeping,

chatting, and playing cards or dominoes. There was a brandy bottle on the table, which seemed to be free to everybody; but this did not tempt me to remain below in an atmosphere which soon became insufferable, so I spent most of the night on deck. The moon shone brightly, and it was worth while sitting up, to see the dark, thickly-wooded banks reflected in the glassy water, and now and then the glow of a charcoal-burner's fire throwing weird shadows among the trees. No sound but the steady splash of the paddle-wheels and the occasional barking of a dog on the lonely shore. Altogether, the circumstances were admirably adapted for reverie and romance, which I indulged in for a time, and then unawares went off to sleep, with my head upon a coil of rope.

When I awoke it was to feel chilly and uncomfortable, and to find that we were in the middle of a thick fog, and in consequence had come to a stand-still. This lasted for some four or five hours, during which the passengers could do nothing but take as long time as possible over their breakfast, and make one another's acquaintance. There were several Englishmen on board the boat. One of them, who certainly did not look like a compatriot, gave me his card, on which he was described as the proprietor of the Garden of Recreation, and director of the Italian Opera House at Monte Video. He informed me that he had been up the river to engage a contralto to sing in 'Norma;' so it seemed that amusements were not neglected in the Banda Oriental, though it was reported to be still in a state of civil war. There were also an English doctor who had been practising and botanizing in Paraguay, and was full of stories of the cruelties of President Lopez, and a traveller, flushed with the triumph of a successful journey over the Andes. Among the steerage passengers were ten prisoners in irons, more like beasts than men. They were a band of desperadoes lately captured in the upper provinces, where they had been assisting the Indians in a raid upon the settlers.

A young Yorkshireman, a new arrival in the country, who was looking about him with the view of buying land, amused us all somewhat by making a great show of a small armoury of various weapons, which he seemed to regard as the most necessary part of his equipment. He evidently imagined himself about to enter upon a very violent and lawless course of life, and informed me with a chuckle, that if any native were to ask him for a light, he would take care to hand it on the point of his revolver. There is nothing like being cautious!

With one of my fellow-travellers I had a very

interesting conversation. He was a New Englander, a fine, tall fellow who might have been a pioneer backwoodsman; but from one or two hints he let drop, I fancy he must have been a preacher of some sort; and he preached me quite an animated little sermon on the state of the country, putting into forcible and sensible words what is pretty much the opinion of most of the Saxon race who have to do with this unlucky people.

'I guess you in England,' he said, 'think that we are wild for republics everywhere. Well, we do think that a well-built republic is one of the strongest and soundest pieces of work on this earth; but you can't build a republic unless you have the materials. The people of this country have tried to imitate our constitution, but they are no more like us than their sun-baked bricks are like our granite rocks, and no amount of flags and fireworks and fine words about liberty and independence will hide the difference. Our ancestors were a hard, gritty kind of folk, who left home for conscience' and justice' sake; theirs came over for greed, hoping to make themselves rich by windfalls of gold and silver, and not by honest labour, which in the long run is the only thing that pays in God's world. They demoralized the country from the beginning; their rule was tyranny, favouritism, and sloth; their religion was all of a piece,—forms and words with which they thought they could please Heaven, while they robbed the poor natives to make offerings to the Virgin, and whipped them at the church doors if they couldn't say their prayers. Nothing good can come of injustice and hypocrisy, and this ignorant, shiftless, stagnant, mongrel race are suffering for the sins of their fathers, and will suffer this good while. They were driven by the folly and weakness of their mother country into proclaiming their independence, as we did; but what good is that to them, or to go on bragging about their twenty-fifth of May, as we do, say you, about our fourth of July? Their republic was only put up to fall to pieces, and ever since that proclamation of independence, the history of the Spanish South American States has been one wearisome story of disputes, factions, jealousies, treacheries, massacres, and revolutions. Not one of them has ever prospered unless it got a little breathing time from its squabbles under the dictatorship of some Francia, or Rosas, or Lopez, who from time to time has managed to seize absolute power, and held on to it as long as he could hang or shoot down all opposition. But after all, they were only Brummagem Napoleons, and not one of them has been able to hand down a settled rule. In this country nothing is certain but uncertainty. Have you ever heard the story told of one of my countrymen, who used to look out of the window every morning and ask the first native he saw what Government they were living under. The answer was, of course, *Quien sabe?* It's a pity, is it? It's a shame, sir. The *gaucho* has good qualities of his own,—qualities so good, that it is a shame to see him at the mercy of the knavish and incapable crew of politicians who have used him to crush the few sensible men that understand the real welfare of the country. But the *gaucho* must be a servant, and not a master. It makes one's blood boil to see that the men who could and should be his masters, the men who are the real bone and sinew of the country, have no voice in its affairs, but must stand by seeing things mismanaged, and labouring for the prosperity of a nation that scarcely thanks them, and would thwart them if it could in their efforts to introduce capital and energy and industry and common sense. But mark my words, sir, this can't last. The foreign settlers, who are trying their best to develope the resources of the country, only ask to be allowed to do this and to live in peace; but if they can't live in peace, they will some day take the matter into their own hands and settle it. If immigration goes on, and if revolution does not go out—why!'—

Here my interlocutor turned abruptly round upon a miserable-looking, barefooted little Argentine soldier, who, attracted by the loud and excited tone of this harangue, had crept near to listen, though he did not understand a word. The New Englander drew himself up to his full height, and looked down on the stunted warrior with such lively disdain, that the poor fellow was quite cowed and shuffled out of the way. 'That's it,' said my friend, and went down to breakfast.

By and by the sun began to clear away the mist, and we were able to move on. By the daylight I could now see the nature of the country through which we were passing. The river is full of islands, which divide it into a great many branches, some of them so narrow and tortuous that it seemed a wonder we did not lose our way. It was strange to steam through these islands, and see the masts of a ship peeping out, apparently in the middle of a copse of trees. The islands, we were told, are still the home of jaguars, which occasionally swim across the current, and astonish the quiet folks on the other side. Some of the passengers said they saw one, but I saw nothing except some huge, long-necked birds, that appeared to enjoy a monopoly of the fishing along the banks. The shore was generally flat, but often it was picturesquely covered with a dense jungle of cactuses, high grasses, and gnarled trees, intermixed with the graceful willow drooping its branches into the stream, and the tall, straight poplar rearing its head above the rest of the luxuriant vegetation. Then again, there would be a long stretch of bare mud and dead flat beyond, fringed, perhaps, with thistle plants of an enormous height; and as we went on, and the river became broader, its banks sometimes rose into high precipitous bluffs, and I caught welcome sight of a low range of hills. Here also we had an opportunity of observing that extraordinary phenomenon, the mirage, which is not uncommon in this climate. The plain by the river bank appeared to be changed into a silvery lake, so real that it was hard to believe it an illusion, and the trees and houses beyond were seen, as it were, floating in the air in a kind of watery light. This lasted for about five minutes.

In the afternoon there was another stoppage, caused by an accident to one of the paddle-wheels. It became pretty certain that we could not reach Buenos Ayres that night, as we were timed to do; but I did not mind, having prudently allowed a day for the delays that might take place in this unpunctual country. It looked like coming on to rain, however; so I accepted the offer of my friend the engineer, and turned in for the night in his cabin. Next morning, when I awoke at sunrise, we were lying in the inner roads of Buenos Ayres, amid a crowd of boats, manned chiefly by jabbering Italians, and out at sea I saw the English flag flying over the mail steamer which was to carry me home.

I took a cab, or coach—a very dilapidated vehicle drawn by two thin horses harnessed promiscuously with bits of cow-hide—to the hotel, and the fare was thirty dollars! But these were paper dollars, the common currency of Buenos Ayres, depreciated at that time, by bad management of the finances, to the value of about twopence each. All the same, I think my driver, like some drivers one has met in other parts of the world, must have been a little extortionate.

The hotel was full of Englishmen, almost all belonging to two classes, camp men and sea-captains, so that little was talked about but sheep and ships. Not finding this conversation very interesting, I strolled out to renew my acquaintance with the town, where I had already spent a few days before going up country.

Buenos Ayres, like other South American cities, is built in squares, chessboard fashion,—an arrangement which does not lend itself to the picturesque, but which is very convenient for the stranger who wishes to find his way. Some of the newer houses are handsome, tall edifices that would not disgrace Paris, but the prevailing pattern is a one-storied, flat-roofed, white-washed square, with a courtyard in the middle, and towards the street, barred windows that hint at insecurity of life and property. When one gets to the suburbs, the country is dotted with the *quintas*, or villas of the foreign merchants, some of which look comfortable enough almost to reconcile the owners to exile. There are not many public buildings. The most striking are the churches with their steeples and domes, the latter covered with bright-coloured tiles. In one of these churches I was shown the flags captured from the English expedition under General Whitelocke,—a sight to make a conceited Briton open his eyes. There are several open squares; the principal one in the middle of the city is called the Plaza de la Victoria. It is lined by a double row of paradise trees, not high enough to give much shade when I saw them; and in the centre stands a statue of republican Liberty, with the inscription, '25th May 1810,' when the people proclaimed their independence of Spain, and fancied they had secured the greatness and prosperity of their country. Here also are the cathedral and the *cabildo* or court-house.

The chief streets are well paved with granite

brought from an island some distance up the river. The whole place is a dead level, till you approach the river, where there is a sudden fall, which must be of great assistance to the drainage of the city. Two moles, built at great expense, stretch far out into the muddy waters of the roads, so shallow that large ships do not approach within several miles, and even boats cannot always be used, which produces the strange spectacle of travellers to this capital city being transferred with their goods, about four or five hundred yards from the shore, to rough carts, and landed thus, as from the bathing machines at Margate. One of these moles seems the liveliest part of the town, affording a cool promenade, and being generally crowded with loungers, children, fruit-vendors, patient anglers, and sailors of all nations carrying baskets of meat and vegetables to the ships. But all the principal streets are lively enough to the eye, except during the hour of *siesta*. One is struck, first by the number of people who in this city go about their business on horseback, and then by the motley collection of tongues, faces, and costumes which meet one everywhere, the population consisting not only of natives of all classes, dignified merchants, and picturesque *gauchos*, but of English, Scotch, Irish,—the last in great numbers,—Italians and Basques, who almost monopolize certain branches of trade, Germans and French,—in fact, representatives of every civilised nation.

There was a feeling of uneasiness, I learned, among this mixed population, especially the foreign part. Rumours were abroad of fresh political disturbance in the provinces, and it was feared that a new revolution might burst forth, as sudden and violent as the Pampero which is the terror of these boundless plains. Such was the not unusual state of affairs that I left behind me, going that same evening on board the packet which was to sail with the next tide.

'What is to be the future of this country?' I said to myself, as I was rowed over the shallow waters of the roads, and saw the sun setting behind the domes and *miradors* of Buenos Ayres—'of this splendid country, where every prospect—where there is any prospect to speak of—pleases, and only man is—unsatisfactory. Will the efforts of its enlightened citizens be hopelessly stifled by the ignorance and apathy of the mass of their countrymen? or are the Argentine States, under happier auspices, destined to become one of the great producing and directing lands of the world, and to flourish in ages to come, when the proverbial New Zealander is photographing the ruins of St. Paul's?'

The church bells of the city ringing across the water, seemed with one voice to be making answer to my unspoken question. And their answer was— *Quien sabe?*

A SELECTION FROM CATALOGUE
OF
Popular and Standard Books
PUBLISHED BY
WILLIAM P. NIMMO, EDINBURGH.

⁎ Complete Catalogue of Mr. Nimmo's Publications, choicely printed and elegantly bound, suitable for the Library, Presentation, and School Prizes, etc. etc., will be forwarded gratis, post free, on application.

'*Mr. Nimmo's books are well known as marvels of cheapness, elegance, and sterling worth.*'—OBSERVER.

NIMMO'S POPULAR EDITION
OF
THE WORKS OF THE POETS.

In fcap. 8vo, printed on toned paper, elegantly bound in cloth extra, with beautifully illuminated imitation ivory tablet on side, price 3s. 6d.; also kept in cloth extra, gilt edges, without tablet; also in full calf, gilt edges, full gilt back; in fine morocco, plain, price 7s. 6d. Each Volume contains a Memoir, and is illustrated with a Portrait of the Author engraved on Steel, and numerous full-page Illustrations on Wood, from designs by eminent Artists; also beautiful Illuminated Title-page.

1. LONGFELLOW'S POETICAL WORKS.
2. SCOTT'S POETICAL WORKS.
3. BYRON'S POETICAL WORKS.
4. MOORE'S POETICAL WORKS.
5. WORDSWORTH'S POETICAL WORKS.

[Continued on next page.

NIMMO'S POPULAR EDITION OF THE WORKS OF THE POETS,

CONTINUED.

---o---

6. COWPER'S POETICAL WORKS.
7. MILTON'S POETICAL WORKS.
8. THOMSON'S POETICAL WORKS.
9. GOLDSMITH'S CHOICE WORKS.
10. POPE'S POETICAL WORKS.
11. BURNS' POETICAL WORKS.
12. THE CASQUET OF GEMS. Choice Selections from the Poets.
13. THE BOOK OF HUMOROUS POETRY.
14. BALLADS: Scottish and English.
15. BUNYAN'S PILGRIM'S PROGRESS AND HOLY WAR.
16. LIVES OF THE BRITISH POETS.
17. THE PROSE WORKS OF ROBERT BURNS.
18. POEMS, SONGS, AND BALLADS OF THE SEA.

*** This Series of Books, from the very superior manner in which it is produced, is at once the cheapest and handsomest edition of the Poets in the market. The volumes form elegant and appropriate Presents as School Prizes and Gift-Books, either in cloth or morocco.

'They are a marvel of cheapness, some of the volumes extending to as many as 700, and even 900, pages, printed on toned paper in a beautifully clear type. Add to this, that they are profusely illustrated with wood engravings, are elegantly and tastefully bound, and that they are published at 3s. 6d. each, and our recommendation of them is complete.'—*Scotsman.*

NIMMO'S SELECT LIBRARY.

―o―

New Series of Choice Books, beautifully printed on superfine paper, profusely Illustrated with original Engravings by the first Artists, and elegantly bound in cloth extra, plain edges, price 3s. 6d. each, or richly bound in cloth and gold, and gilt edges, price 5s. each.

THIRD EDITION.

1. **Almost Faultless:** A Story of the Present Day. By the Author of 'A Book for Governesses.'

'The author has written a capital story in a high moral tone.'—*The Court Journal.*

SECOND EDITION.

2. **Lives of Old English Worthies before the Conquest.** By W. H. DAVENPORT ADAMS.

'The author's aim is to illuminate, what may be regarded as obscure, certain periods of historic England, accompanied with biographical sketches.'—*Courant.*

SECOND EDITION.

3. **Every-Day Objects; or, Picturesque Aspects of Natural** History. By W. H. DAVENPORT ADAMS.

FIFTH EDITION.

4. **My Schoolboy Friends:** A Story of Whitminster Grammar School. By ASCOTT R. HOPE, Author of 'A Book about Dominies,' 'Stories of School Life,' etc.

'This is a most interesting book. Boys, for whom it is especially written, will thoroughly enjoy it.'—*Westminster Review.*

SECOND EDITION.

5. **Drifted and Sifted:** A Domestic Chronicle of the Seventeenth Century.

'The author of this interesting, and we may add pathetic, story appears to possess the art of reproducing bygone times with much ability.'—*The Record.*

6. **Warrior, Priest, and Statesman; or, English Heroes in the** Thirteenth Century. By W. H. DAVENPORT ADAMS.

7. **Totty Testudo.** The Life and Wonderful Adventures of Totty Testudo. An Autobiography by FLORA F. WYLDE.

'The book is of engrossing interest, and the reader will be astonished, as he lays it down, to find that he has been able to get so much entertainment and instruction from the personal adventures of a tortoise.'—*Inverness Courier.*

8. **On Holy Ground; or, Scenes and Incidents in the Land** of Promise. By EDWIN HODDER, Author of 'Memories of New Zealand Life,' 'The Junior Clerk,' etc.

NIMMO'S CROWN GIFT BOOKS.

Crown 8vo, beautifully printed on superfine paper, profusely Illustrated by eminent Artists, in cloth extra, plain edges, price 3s. 6d. each, or richly bound in cloth and gold, and gilt edges, price 5s. each.

THIRD EDITION.

1. **Sword and Pen; or, English Worthies in the Reign of Elizabeth.** By W. H. DAVENPORT ADAMS.

'A more *wholesome* book for young readers we have seldom seen.'—*The Athenæum.*

SECOND EDITION.

2. **Norrie Seton; or, Driven to Sea.** By Mrs. George Cupples, Author of 'Unexpected Pleasures,' etc.

'Mrs. Cupples has given to the boys in this volume just the sort of sea-story with which they will be delighted.'—*The Scotsman.*

SECOND EDITION.

3. **The Circle of the Year; or, Studies of Nature and Pictures of the Seasons.** By W. H. DAVENPORT ADAMS.

'Its purpose is to tell both young and old, but especially the former, how much of interest there is in everything connected with Nature.'—*Bell's Messenger.*

SECOND EDITION.

4. **The Wealth of Nature: Our Food Supplies from the Vegetable Kingdom.** By the Rev. JOHN MONTGOMERY, A.M.

'It would be difficult to put into the hands of any boy or girl a volume which more equally combines the instructive and interesting in literature.'—*N. B. Mail.*

FIFTH EDITION.

5. **Stories of School Life.** By Ascott R. Hope.

6. **Stories of French School Life.** By Ascott R. Hope.

'We were among the many who greatly admired Mr. Hope's "Stories of School Life" and "Stories about Boys," and when we found that he had undertaken to illustrate French school life, we gladly opened the volume. The stories are interesting in the highest degree; they appeal to the best sympathies of the lads for whom they are written. They set forth the right and the true against the false, and they are full of good, hearty humour.'—*Public Opinion.*

NIMMO'S UNIVERSAL GIFT BOOKS.

A Series of excellent Works, profusely Illustrated with original Engravings by the first Artists, choicely printed on superfine paper, and elegantly bound in cloth and gold, and gilt edges, crown 8vo, price 3s. 6d. each.

1. Tales of Old English Life; or, Pictures of the Periods. By WILLIAM FRANCIS COLLIER, LL.D., Author of 'History of English Literature,' etc.
2. Mungo Park's Life and Travels. With a Supplementary Chapter, detailing the results of recent Discovery in Africa.
3. Benjamin Franklin: A Biography. From the celebrated 'Life' by JARED SPARKS, and the more recent and extensive 'Life and Times' by JAMES PARTON.
4. Wallace, the Hero of Scotland: A Biography. By JAMES PATERSON.
5. Men of History. By Eminent Writers.
6. Women of History. By Eminent Writers.
7. Old-World Worthies; or, Classical Biography. Selected from PLUTARCH'S LIVES.
8. Epoch Men, and the Results of their Lives. By Samuel NEIL.
9. The Mirror of Character. Selected from the Writings of OVERBURY, EARLE, and BUTLER.
10. Wisdom, Wit, and Allegory. Selected from 'The Spectator.'
11. The Spanish Inquisition: Its Heroes and Martyrs. By JANET GORDON, Author of 'Champions of the Reformation,' etc.
12. The Improvement of the Mind. By Isaac Watts, D.D.
13. The Man of Business considered in Six Aspects. A Book for Young Men.

*** This elegant and useful Series of Books has been specially prepared for School and College Prizes: they are, however, equally suitable for General Presentation. In selecting the works for this Series, the aim of the Publisher has been to produce books of a permanent value, interesting in manner and instructive in matter—books that youth will read eagerly and with profit, and which will be found equally attractive in after-life.

Books published by William P. Nimmo,

NIMMO'S ALL THE YEAR ROUND GIFT BOOKS.

A series of entertaining and instructive volumes, profusely Illustrated with original Engravings by the first Artists, choicely printed on superfine paper, and elegantly bound in cloth and gold, and gilt edges, crown 8vo, price 3s. 6d. each.

1. Christian Osborne's Friends. By Mrs. Harriet Miller Davidson, Author of 'Isobel Jardine's History,' and Daughter of the late Hugh Miller.
2. Round the Grange Farm; or, Good Old Times. By Jean L. Watson, Author of 'Bygone Days in our Village,' etc.
3. Stories about Boys. By Ascott R. Hope, Author of 'Stories of School Life,' 'My Schoolboy Friends,' etc. etc.
4. George's Enemies: A Sequel to 'My Schoolboy Friends.' By Ascott R. Hope, Author of 'Stories about Boys,' etc. etc.
5. Violet Rivers; or, Loyal to Duty. A Tale for Girls. By Winifred Taylor, Author of 'Story of Two Lives,' etc.
6. Wild Animals and Birds: Curious and Instructive Stories about their Habits and Sagacity. With numerous Illustrations.
7. The Twins of Saint-Marcel: A Tale of Paris Incendie. By Mrs. A. S. Orr, Author of 'The Roseville Family,' etc. etc.
8. Rupert Rochester, the Banker's Son. A Tale. By Winifred Taylor, Author of 'Story of Two Lives,' etc.
9. The Story of Two Lives; or, The Trials of Wealth and Poverty. By Winifred Taylor, Author of 'Rupert Rochester,' etc.
10. The Lost Father; or, Cecilia's Triumph. A Story of our own Day. By Daryl Holme.
11. Friendly Fairies; or, Once upon a Time.
12. The Young Mountaineer; or, Frank Miller's Lot in Life. The Story of a Swiss Boy. By Daryl Holme.
13. Stories from over the Sea. With Illustrations.
14. The Story of a Noble Life; or, Zurich and its Reformer Ulric Zwingle. By Mrs. Hardy (Janet Gordon), Author of 'The Spanish Inquisition,' 'Champions of the Reformation,' etc. etc.
15. Stories of Whitminster. By Ascott R. Hope, Author of 'My Schoolboy Friends,' 'Stories about Boys,' etc. etc.

*** The object steadily kept in view in preparing the above series has been to give a collection of works of a thoroughly healthy moral tone, agreeably blending entertainment and instruction. It is believed this end has been attained, and that the several volumes will be found eminently suitable as Gift Books and School Prizes, besides proving of permanent value in the Home Library.

NIMMO'S HALF-CROWN REWARD BOOKS.

Extra foolscap 8vo, cloth elegant, gilt edges, Illustrated, price 2s. 6d. each.

1. Memorable Wars of Scotland. By Patrick Fraser Tytler, F.R.S.E., Author of 'The History of Scotland,' etc.
2. Seeing the World: A Young Sailor's own Story. By CHARLES NORDHOFF, Author of 'The Young Man-of-War's-Man.'
3. The Martyr Missionary: Five Years in China. By Rev. CHARLES P. BUSH, M.A.
4. My New Home: A Woman's Diary.
5. Home Heroines: Tales for Girls. By T. S. Arthur, Author of 'Life's Crosses,' etc.
6. Lessons from Women's Lives. By Sarah J. Hale.
7. The Roseville Family. A Historical Tale of the Eighteenth Century. By Mrs. A. S. ORR, Author of 'Mountain Patriots,' etc.
8. Leah. A Tale of Ancient Palestine. Illustrative of the Story of Naaman the Syrian. By Mrs. A. S. ORR.
9. Champions of the Reformation: The Stories of their Lives. By JANET GORDON.
10. The History of Two Wanderers; or, Cast Adrift.
11. Beattie's Poetical Works.
12. The Vicar of Wakefield. By Oliver Goldsmith.
13. Edgar Allan Poe's Poetical Works.
14. The Miner's Son, and Margaret Vernon. By M. M. POLLARD, Author of 'The Minister's Daughter,' etc. etc.
15. How Frank began to Climb the Ladder, and the Friends who lent him a hand. By CHARLES BRUCE, Author of 'Lame Felix,' etc.
16. Conrad and Columbine. A Fairy Tale. By James MASON.
17. Aunt Ann's Stories. Edited by Louisa Loughborough.
18. The Snow-Sweepers' Party, and the Tale of Old Tubbins. By R. ST. JOHN CORBET, Author of 'Mince Pie Island,' etc. etc.
19. The Story of Elise Marcel. A Tale for Girls.

Books published by William P. Nimmo,

NIMMO'S
Two Shilling Reward Books.

Foolscap 8vo, Illustrated, elegantly bound in cloth extra, bevelled boards, gilt back and side, gilt edges, price 2s. each.

1. The Far North: Explorations in the Arctic Regions. By ELISHA KENT KANE, M.D.
2. Great Men of European History. From the Beginning of the Christian Era till the Present Time. By DAVID PRYDE, M.A.
3. The Young Men of the Bible. A Series of Papers, Biographical and Suggestive. By Rev. JOSEPH A. COLLIER.
4. The Blade and the Ear: A Book for Young Men.
5. Monarchs of Ocean: Columbus and Cook.
6. Life's Crosses, and How to Meet them. By T. S. Arthur.
7. A Father's Legacy to his Daughters, etc. A Book for Young Women. By Dr. GREGORY.
8. Mountain Patriots. A Tale of the Reformation in Savoy. By Mrs. A. S. ORR.
9. Labours of Love: A Tale for the Young. By Winifred Taylor.
10. Mossdale: A Tale for the Young. By Anna M. De Iongh.
11. The Standard-Bearer. A Tale of the Times of Constantine the Great. By ELLEN PALMER.
12. Jacqueline. A Story of the Reformation in Holland. By Mrs. HARDY (JANET GORDON).

NIMMO'S
Home and School Reward Books.

Foolscap 8vo, Illustrated, elegantly bound in cloth extra, bevelled boards, gilt back and side, gilt edges, price 2s. each.

1. Lame Felix. A Book for Boys. By Charles Bruce.
2. Picture Lessons by the Divine Teacher; or, Illustrations of the Parables of our Lord. By PETER GRANT, D.D.
3. Nonna: A Story of the Days of Julian the Apostate. By Ellen Palmer.
4. Philip Walton; or, Light at Last. By the Author of 'Meta Frantz,' etc.
5. The Minister's Daughter, and Old Anthony's Will. Tales for the Young. By M. M. POLLARD, Author of 'The Miner's Son,' etc. etc.
6. The Two Sisters. By M. M. Pollard.
7. A Needle and Thread: A Tale for Girls. By Emma J. Barnes, Author of 'Faithful and True, or the Mother's Legacy.'
8. Taken Up: A Tale for Boys and Girls. By A. Whymper.
9. An Earl's Daughter. By M. M. Pollard.
10. Life at Hartwell; or, Frank and his Friends. By Katharine E. MAY, Author of 'Alfred and his Mother,' etc. etc.
11. Stories Told in a Fisherman's Cottage. By Ellen Palmer, Author of 'Nonna,' 'The Standard-Bearer,' etc. etc.
12. Max Wild, the Merchant's Son; and other Stories for the Young.

NIMMO'S
Sunday-School Reward Books.

Foolscap 8vo, cloth extra, gilt edges, Illustrated, price 1s. 6d. each.

1. Bible Blessings.   By Rev. Richard Newton.
2. One Hour a Week: Fifty-two Bible Lessons for the Young.
3. The Best Things.   By Rev. Richard Newton.
4. The Story of John Heywood: A Tale of the Time of Harry VIII. By CHARLES BRUCE, Author of 'How Frank began to Climb,' etc.
5. Lessons from Rose Hill; and Little Nannette.
6. Great and Good Women: Biographies for Girls. By LYDIA H. SIGOURNEY.
7. At Home and Abroad; or, Uncle William's Adventures.
8. Alfred and his Mother; or, Seeking the Kingdom. By KATHARINE E. MAY.
9. Asriel; or, The Crystal Cup. By Mrs. Henderson.
10. The Kind Governess; or, How to make Home Happy.
11. Percy and Ida.   By Katharine E. May.
12. Three Wet Sundays with the Book of Joshua. By Ellen PALMER, Author of 'Christmas at the Beacon,' etc. etc.
13. The Fishermen of Galilee; or, Sunday Talks with Papa. By ELLEN PALMER.

NIMMO'S
Sunday and Week-Day Reward Books.

Foolscap 8vo, cloth extra, gilt edges, Illustrated, price 1s. 6d. each.

1. The Sculptor of Bruges.   By Mrs. W. G. Hall.
2. From Cottage to Castle; or, Faithful in Little. A Tale founded on Fact. By M. H., Author of 'The Red Velvet Bible,' etc.
3. Christmas at the Beacon.   By Ellen Palmer.
4. The Sea and the Savages: A Story of Adventure. By HAROLD LINCOLN.
5. The Swedish Singer; or, The Story of Vanda Rosendahl. By Mrs. W. G. HALL.
6. My Beautiful Home; or, Lily's Search. By Chas. Bruce.
7. The Story of a Moss Rose; or, Ruth and the Orphan Family. By CHARLES BRUCE.
8. Summer Holidays at Silversea.   By E. Rosalie Salmon.
9. Fred Graham's Resolve.   By the Author of 'Mat and Sofie.'
10. Wilton School; or, Harry Campbell's Revenge. A Tale. By F. E. WEATHERLY.
11. Grace Harvey and her Cousins.
12. Blind Mercy; and other Tales.   By Gertrude Crockford.
13. Evan Lindsay. By Margaret Fraser Tytler, Author of 'Tales of Good and Great Kings,' 'Tales of the Great and Brave,' etc.

Nimmo's One Shilling Favourite Reward Books.

Demy 18mo, Illustrated, cloth extra, price 1s. each; also in gilt side and edges, price 1s. 6d. each.

1. **The Vicar of Wakefield.** Poems and Essays. By OLIVER GOLDSMITH.
2. **Æsop's Fables, with Instructive Applications.** By Dr. CROXALL.
3. **Bunyan's Pilgrim's Progress.**
4. **The Young Man-of-War's-Man:** A Boy's Voyage round the World. By CHARLES NORDHOFF.
5. **The Treasury of Anecdote:** Moral and Religious.
6. **The Boy's Own Workshop;** or, The Young Carpenters. By JACOB ABBOTT.
7. **The Life and Adventures of Robinson Crusoe.**
8. **The History of Sandford and Merton.** A Moral and Instructive Lesson for Young Persons.
9. **Evenings at Home; or, The Juvenile Budget Opened.** Consisting of a variety of Miscellaneous Pieces for the Instruction and Amusement of Young Persons. By Dr. AIKIN and Mrs. BARBAULD.
10. **Unexpected Pleasures; or, Left alone in the Holidays.** By Mrs. GEORGE CUPPLES, Author of 'Norrie Seton,' etc.
11. **The Beauties of Shakespeare.** With a General Index by the Rev. WILLIAM DODD, LL.D.
12. **Gems from 'The Spectator.'** A Selection from the most admired Writings of Addison and Steele.
13. **Burns' Poetical Works.** With a Complete Glossary.
14. **The Sketch Book.** By WASHINGTON IRVING.

⁎ The above Series of elegant and useful books is specially prepared for the entertainment and instruction of young persons.

Nimmo's Popular Religious Gift Books.

18mo, finely printed on toned paper, handsomely bound in cloth extra, price 1s. each.

1. **Across the River: Twelve Views of Heaven.** By Norman MACLEOD, D.D.; R. W. HAMILTON, D.D.; ROBERT S. CANDLISH, D.D.; JAMES HAMILTON, D.D.; etc. etc.
2. **Emblems of Jesus; or, Illustrations of Emmanuel's Character and Work.**
3. **Life Thoughts of Eminent Christians.**
4. **Comfort for the Desponding; or, Words to Soothe and Cheer Troubled Hearts.**
5. **The Chastening of Love: Words of Consolation for the Christian Mourner.** By JOSEPH PARKER, D.D., Manchester.
6. **The Cedar Christian, and other Practical Papers.** By the Rev. THEODORE L. CUYLER.
7. **Consolation for Christian Mothers Bereaved of Little Children.** By A FRIEND OF MOURNERS.
8. **The Orphan; or, Words of Comfort for the Fatherless and Motherless.**
9. **Gladdening Streams; or, The Waters of the Sanctuary.** A Book for Fragments of Time on each Lord's Day of the Year.
10. **Spirit of the Old Divines.**
11. **Choice Gleanings from Sacred Writers.**
12. **Direction in Prayer; or, The Lord's Prayer Illustrated in a Series of Expositions.** By PETER GRANT, D.D.
13. **Scripture Imagery.** By Peter Grant, D.D., Author of 'Emblems of Jesus,' etc.

NIMMO'S ONE SHILLING ILLUSTRATED JUVENILE BOOKS.

Foolscap 8vo, Coloured Frontispieces, handsomely bound in cloth, Illuminated, price 1s. each.

1. **Four Little People and their Friends.**
2. **Elizabeth; or, The Exiles of Siberia. A Tale** from the French of Madame COTTIN.
3. **Paul and Virginia. From the French of** BERNARDIN SAINT-PIERRE.
4. **Little Threads: Tangle Thread, Golden** Thread, and Silver Thread.
5. **Benjamin Franklin, the Printer Boy.**
6. **Barton Todd, and The Young Lawyer.**
7. **The Perils of Greatness: The Story of Alex**ander Menzikoff.
8. **Little Crowns, and How to Win them. By** Rev. JOSEPH A. COLLIER.
9. **Great Riches: Nelly Rivers' Story. By Aunt** FANNY.
10. **The Right Way, and The Contrast.**
11. **The Daisy's First Winter. And other Stories.** By HARRIET BEECHER STOWE.
12. **The Man of the Mountain. And other** Stories.
13. **Better than Rubies. Stories for the Young,** Illustrative of Familiar Proverbs. With 62 Illustrations.

[*Continued on next page.*

NIMMO'S ONE SHILLING ILLUSTRATED JUVENILE BOOKS,
CONTINUED.

14. **Experience Teaches.** And other Stories for the Young, Illustrative of Familiar Proverbs. With 39 Illustrations.
15. **The Happy Recovery.** And other Stories for the Young. With 26 Illustrations.
16. **Gratitude and Probity.** And other Stories for the Young. With 21 Illustrations.
17. **The Two Brothers.** And other Stories for the Young. With 13 Illustrations.
18. **The Young Orator.** And other Stories for the Young. With 9 Illustrations.
19. **Simple Stories to Amuse and Instruct Young Readers.** With Illustrations.
20. **The Three Friends.** And other Stories for the Young. With Illustrations.
21. **Sybil's Sacrifice.** And other Stories for the Young. With 12 Illustrations.
22. **The Old Shepherd.** And other Stories for the Young. With Illustrations.
23. **The Young Officer.** And other Stories for the Young. With Illustrations.
24. **The False Heir.** And other Stories for the Young. With Illustrations.
25. **The Old Farmhouse; or, Alice Morton's Home.** And other Stories. By M. M. POLLARD.
26. **Twyford Hall; or, Rosa's Christmas Dinner, and what she did with it.** By CHARLES BRUCE.
27. **The Discontented Weathercock.** And other Stories for Children. By M. JONES.
28. **Out at Sea, and other Stories.** By Two Authors.
29. **The Story of Waterloo; or, The Fall of NAPOLEON.**
30. **Sister Jane's Little Stories.** Edited by Louisa LOUGHBOROUGH.

NIMMO'S
NINEPENNY SERIES FOR BOYS AND GIRLS.

In demy 18mo, with Illustrations, elegantly bound in cloth.

This Series of Books will be found unequalled for genuine interest and value, and it is believed they will be eagerly welcomed by thoughtful children of both sexes. Parents may rest assured that each Volume teaches some noble lesson, or enforces some valuable truth.

1. In the Brave Days of Old ; or, The Story of the Spanish Armada. For Boys and Girls.
2. The Lost Ruby. By the Author of 'The Basket of Flowers,' etc.
3. Leslie Ross ; or, Fond of a Lark. By Charles Bruce.
4. My First and Last Voyage. By Benjamin Clarke.
5. Little Katie: A Fairy Story. By Charles Bruce.
6. Being Afraid. And other Stories for the Young. By Charles Stuart.
7. The Toll-Keepers. And other Stories for the Young. By Benjamin Clarke.
8. Dick Barford: A Boy who would go down Hill. By Charles Bruce.
9. Joan of Arc ; or, The Story of a Noble Life. Written for Girls.
10. Helen Siddal: A Story for Children. By Ellen Palmer.
11. Mat and Sofie: A Story for Boys and Girls.
12. Peace and War. By the Author of 'The Basket of Flowers,' etc.
13. Perilous Adventures of a French Soldier in Algeria.
14. The Magic Glass ; or, The Secret of Happiness.
15. Hawks' Dene: A Tale for Children. By Katharine E. May.
16. Little Maggie. And other Stories. By the Author of 'The Joy of Well-Doing,' etc. etc.
17. The Brother's Legacy ; or, Better than Gold. By M. M. Pollard.
18. The Little Sisters ; or, Jealousy. And other Stories for the Young. By the Author of 'Little Tales for Tiny Tots,' etc.
19. Kate's New Home. By Cecil Scott, Author of 'Chryssie Lyle,' etc.

NEW WORKS.

NEW EDITION OF THE EDINA BURNS.

In crown 4to, price 12s. 6d., elegantly bound in cloth, extra gilt and gilt edges, also in Turkey morocco antique, very handsome, 42s., the popular Drawing-room Edition of the

Poems and Songs by Robert Burns. With Illustrations by R. HERDMAN, WALLER H. PATON, SAM. BOUGH, GOURLAY STEELL, D. O. HILL, J. M'WHIRTER, and other eminent Scottish Artists.

Fourth Edition. Eleventh Thousand.

In demy 8vo, cloth elegant, richly gilt, price 7s. 6d., or in Turkey morocco antique, 21s.,

Things a Lady would Like to Know, concerning Domestic Management and Expenditure, arranged for Daily Reference. By HENRY SOUTHGATE, Author of 'Many Thoughts of Many Minds,' 'Noble Thoughts in Noble Language,' 'Gone Before,' 'The Bridal Bouquet,' etc. etc.

Tenth Thousand.

In crown 8vo, beautifully bound in cloth extra, full of Engravings and Coloured Pictures, price 3s. 6d., or gilt edges price 4s.,

Three Hundred Bible Stories and Three Hundred Bible Pictures. A Pictorial Sunday Book for the Young.

The Excelsior Edition of Shakespeare's Complete Works.

In large demy 8vo, with Steel Portrait and Vignette, handsomely bound, price 5s.,

Shakespeare's Complete Works. With a Biographical Sketch by MARY COWDEN CLARKE, a Copious Glossary, and numerous Illustrations.

The Excelsior Edition of Whiston's Josephus.

In large demy 8vo, with Steel Portrait and Vignette, handsomely bound, price 5s.,

The Whole Works of Flavius Josephus, the Jewish Historian. With Life, Portrait, Notes, Index, etc.

THE WAVERLEY NOVELS.

ENTIRELY NEW EDITION.

Crown 8vo, with Frontispiece and Vignette, in elegant wrapper printed in colours, price 1s. each. Also, in Twenty-six volumes, cloth extra, full gilt back, price 2s. per volume; and in Thirteen double volumes, roxburgh style, gilt top, price 3s. 6d. per volume.

Edited by the Rev. P. HATELY WADDELL, LL.D. With Notes, Biographical and Critical, and a Glossary of Scotch Words and Foreign Phrases for each Novel.

1. Waverley; or, ''Tis Sixty Years Since.'
2. Guy Mannering; or, The Astrologer.
3. The Antiquary.
4. Rob Roy.
5. Old Mortality.
6. The Black Dwarf, and A Legend of Montrose.
7. The Bride of Lammermoor.
8. The Heart of Mid-Lothian.
9. Ivanhoe: A Romance.
10. The Monastery.
11. The Abbot: A Sequel.
12. Kenilworth.
13. The Pirate.
14. The Fortunes of Nigel.
15. Peveril of the Peak.
16. Quentin Durward.
17. St. Ronan's Well.
18. Redgauntlet.
19. The Betrothed.
20. The Talisman: A Tale of the Crusaders.
21. Woodstock; or, The Cavalier.
22. The Fair Maid of Perth; or, St. Valentine's Day.
23. Anne of Geierstein; or, The Maiden of the Mist.
24. Count Robert of Paris.
25. The Surgeon's Daughter, and Castle Dangerous.
26. The Highland Widow, and my Aunt Margaret's Mirror.
    With an interesting summarised account of the Scott Centenary.

The above may also be had in substantial half-calf bindings.

NIMMO'S NATIONAL LIBRARY.

Just ready, in crown 8vo, with Steel Frontispiece and Vignette, handsomely bound, cloth extra, price 5s. each; also in full gilt side, back, and edges, price 6s. each.

Seventh Thousand.

The English Circumnavigators: The most re-markable Voyages round the World by English Sailors. (Drake, Dampier, Anson, and Cook's Voyages.) With a Preliminary Sketch of their Lives and Discoveries. Edited, with Notes, Maps, etc., by DAVID LAING PURVES and R. COCHRANE.

The Book of Adventure and Peril. A Record of Heroism and Endurance on Sea and Land. Compiled and Edited by CHARLES BRUCE, Editor of 'Sea Songs and Ballads,' 'The Birthday Book of Proverbs,' etc.

The Great Triumphs of Great Men. Edited by JAMES MASON. Illustrated.

Great Historical Mutinies, comprising the Story of the Mutiny of the 'Bounty,' the Mutiny at Spithead and the Nore, the Mutinies of the Highland Regiments, and the Indian Mutiny, etc. Edited by DAVID HERBERT, M.A.

Famous Historical Scenes from Three Conturies. Pictures of celebrated events from the Reformation to the end of the French Revolution. Selected from the works of Standard Authors by A. R. HOPE MONCRIEFF.

The English Explorers; comprising details of the more famous Travels by Mandeville, Bruce, Park, and Livingstone. With Map of Africa and Chapter on Arctic Exploration.

The Book for Every Day; containing an In-exhaustible Store of Amusing and Instructive Articles. Edited by JAMES MASON.

The Book of Noble Englishwomen: Lives made Illustrious by Heroism, Goodness, and Great Attainments. Edited by CHARLES BRUCE.

A Hundred Wonders of the World in Nature and Art, described according to the latest Authorities, and profusely Illustrated. Edited by JOHN SMALL, M.A.

Other Popular and Standard Volumes in preparation.

www.ingramcontent.com/pod-product-compliance
Lightning Source LLC
Chambersburg PA
CBHW030316240426
43673CB00040B/1183